Elementary Composition Practice:
Book 2

A Text for Students of English as a Second Language

Linda Lonon Blanton
Central YMCA Community College
Chicago, Illinois

Newbury House Publishers, Inc.
Rowley, Massachusetts 01969

Library of Congress Cataloging in Publication Data (Revised)

Blanton, Linda Lonon, 1942-
    Elementary composition practice.

    1. English language--Text-books for foreigners.
2. English language--Composition and exercises.
I. Title.
PE1128.B59   428'.2'4   78-5736
ISBN 0-88377-128-4 (bk. 2)

NEWBURY HOUSE PUBLISHERS, INC.

 Language Science
Language Teaching
Language Learning

ROWLEY, MASSACHUSETTS 01969

Artwork by Barbara Frake.

Printed in the U.S.A.

First printing: February 1979
12

Preface

Elementary Composition Practice: Book 2 has grown out of materials developed for an intensive beginning reading and composition course for adult learners of English as a second language. Book 2 is a composition text designed for students on a high elementary or low intermediate level, although it is realized that the terms "elementary" and "intermediate" may vary from program to program. *Elementary Composition Practice: Book 1,* the lead book in the series, is considered to be the first composition book adults learning English would work through; Book 2 follows, expands, and reinforces the lessons contained in Book 1. It is hoped that teachers and administrators who are considering the texts will look at the level of content, regardless of the label used for students studying on that level in their individual programs. The book titles are intended as guides, not definitions.

The materials contained in ECP: Book 2 are not self-instructional; they presume the presence of a professional teacher. A section following the Table of Contents, entitled "To the Teacher," gives suggestions as to how the materials might be used effectively. Anyone using or contemplating use of the materials is urged to read that section.

ECP: Book 2 is divided into ten units. Each unit contains an illustrated reading passage, followed by exercises on comprehension, grammar, vocabulary, textual cohesion, order, or writing mechanics. Notes and questions on the organization of the reading passage, designed to help the teacher lead the students in discussion, lead into a model composition, which makes use of the vocabulary, grammatical structures, and organizational framework of the reading passage. Students are then presented with detailed instructions for writing their own compositions. All reading passages and model compositions focus on certain kinds of composition writing, such as narration and description, and certain manners of organization, such as chronological order, spatial order, and classification.

The assumption behind these materials is that there is more to writing on even an elementary level than unconnected sentence exercises. It is felt that beginning students can understand and practice sophisticated principles and techniques of English composition writing without waiting until they know more English. The strict criterion is that these techniques and principles be presented simply and methodically. It is felt that both Book 1 and Book 2 adhere to that criterion.

Preface

I wish to thank ESL/EFL colleagues, both local and worldwide, who have responded with support and valuable criticism to ECP: Book 1 and with encouragement for the continuation of the series. Their attention is greatly appreciated.

L. L. B.

Contents

Contents

Contents

Elementary Composition Practice: Book 2

To the teacher

The materials contained within *Elementary Composition Practice* are based on the presupposition that elementary English language students can indeed write compositions, not just do writing-type exercises, as long as they are allowed, in preparation for writing their compositions, to become familiar with organizational and situational frameworks and are supplied with vocabulary and grammatical structures to manipulate within those frameworks. The methodology involves creating an awareness of different modes of organization which lend themselves to the ordering of different kinds of data in English. For example, details of a person's daily life lend themselves well to chronological ordering. In addition, students must learn the structure vocabulary, i.e., vocabulary for expressing relationships, which the language provides for ordering within a particular organizational framework. For example, data ordered chronologically can be tied together with *first, next, afterwards,* etc. It is assumed that this approach will make students better writers and readers, for data in the new language will no longer appear in a formless mass.

Elementary Composition Practice: Book 2 is designed for students of English as a second language of high elementary or low intermediate levels of proficiency. It is intended for adults who want to learn English for professional, academic, and business reasons. The format, as well as some of the actual lessons, have been tested successfully with students ranging in age from 15 to 55, from nine different language backgrounds and of educational backgrounds ranging from ninth grade to university degrees. The text provides 40-50 class hours of instruction (an intensive 8-10 week course).

ECP: Book 2 is divided into ten units, each containing an illustrated reading passage, exercises on the reading, a model composition, and instructions for the student's composition. The instructions accompanying each exercise are written as simply as possible, yet in some cases may need further oral explanation. The notes and questions on the organization of each preceding reading passage, to be found at the end of the exercise section in each unit, are intended for the teacher's use in guiding students, in oral discussion, toward a conscious understanding of the functional nature of paragraphing (to introduce the topic, to discuss the topic, to conclude the topic) and the ordering of information within those paragraphs (chronological order, spatial order, classification, etc.).

The readings, each with a companion model set within the same organizational and situational framework, progress in grammatical difficulty, on the sentence level, from the simple present tense to the present continuous tense to the future with **be going to** to the simple past to the present perfect, with modals interspersed along the way. This progression was chosen because the lessons in beginning grammar classes are often so ordered and it was assumed that students using ECP: Book 2 would be studying grammar separately and simultaneously. If that is not the case, the teacher could build grammatical explanations, examples, and more grammar-based exercises into each unit.

The exercises following each reading are varied for the sake of not boring the students, as well as covering more ground over the entire text. The notion of *cohesion* is introduced in the exercises and can be explained simply as the "glue" that holds ideas together, sometimes within sentences, sometimes across sentences. As students do the exercises on *reference* and *connection,* both of which help to provide cohesion, they will begin to understand the concept.

The model composition in each unit makes use of the grammatical structures, vocabulary, and organization of the reading passage. It is a shorter, simpler version of the reading passage and serves as the immediate resource for the student's ensuing composition. Students should not copy the model, but rather use its ideas, grammatical structures, vocabulary, etc., to create their own compositions.

An attempt was made in all reading passages and model compositions to make the content realistic by focusing on people like any of us who work and play and study. Specific places are mentioned, but the locale should be unimportant for the comprehension of the readings and students will substitute their own environments in their writing. It is felt that this personalization of the topic facilitates writing competence.

The instructions for the student's own composition at the end of each unit should be interpreted and explained by the teacher. The teacher should closely supervise to see that these instructions are understood and followed. Each entire unit is designed to prepare the student for the composition which, in a sense, culminates the unit. The purpose of what precedes each composition is to provide the student with the mind-set within which to create his own composition and the linguistic tools with which to do so. The diagram at the end of each page of "Instructions for the student's composition" is there to give a visual image of the shape of the composition in terms of paragraphs. Simply drawing boxes on the blackboard and talking about what goes in each "box" is often helpful as part of a pre-composition discussion. In some diagrams, the label "Body" is used, while in others, it is not. Where it is not used, the conclusion of the preceding reading passage and model composition is not a separate component which follows the body. Instead, the contents are organized so that the final paragraph of the body serves as the conclusion to the composition. That dual function is something which students will understand as they work through the "Notes and questions on the organization of the reading" in each unit.

The pictures which illustrate the reading passage in each unit can be used for oral and written composition. The teacher can read the "story," while students follow the meaning in the pictures. Additional composition practice in each unit could come from having students write what they see in the pictures.

The readings and models are primarily descriptive (Units 3, 4, 9) and narrative (Units 1, 5, 7, 10) in type. Units 2 and 6 are in letter form: Unit 2, a friendly letter, and Unit 6, a business letter. Unit 8 is expository. Six different organizational frameworks are presented and are either used singly or in combination:

Chronological order (a time arrangement): Units 1, 4, 5, 7
Classification (a narrowing subject focus): Units 3, 8, 9, 10
Spatial order (a space arrangement): Unit 2
Shift of focus (from one subject to another, all tied to the speaker): Unit 2
Ranking (a hierarchical arrangement): Unit 6
Balance of contrasts (equalization of focus): Unit 9

Students should be made consciously aware of these frameworks as they progress through the materials. Diagrams are often useful for a visual grasp of the organizational concepts:

Chronological order: 1 | time   *Example*: 9:00, 9:30, 9:45
                       2 |
                       3 ↓

Classification: [   ]   *Example*: the weather, divided in-
                  [ ] [ ] [ ] [ ]   to fall, spring, summer, winter

To the teacher

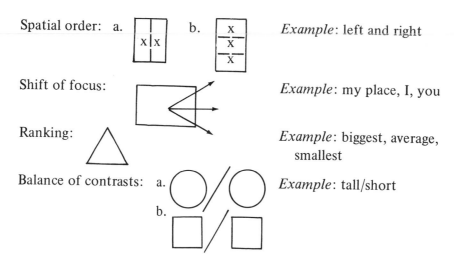

Spatial order: a. [diagram] b. [diagram]   *Example*: left and right

Shift of focus: [diagram]   *Example*: my place, I, you

Ranking: [diagram]   *Example*: biggest, average, smallest

Balance of contrasts: a. [diagram]   *Example*: tall/short
b. [diagram]

Each unit is designed to provide material for five hours of class work. If students meet for composition five days a week, in an intensive program, all of the basic work can be done in class. If they meet fewer days per week, the exercises can be assigned as homework and one unit can still be completed in a week's time.

The following is a five-day suggested breakdown of each unit:

Day 1: *Reading*

The teacher presents the content of the reading orally several times, as if telling a story. Students listen, following along with the pictures. Next, the teacher reads the text aloud, while students follow, reading silently. New words and grammatical structures are explained. Students then read silently again, using dictionaries to recheck any problem vocabulary. The teacher next asks questions about the reading which students answer by finding the sentence where the answer appears and reading it aloud. Then, the teacher writes sequential questions about the reading on the board. Students are called on to retell the text by answering the questions without reference to the book. (The teacher may want to omit some of these steps as the proficiency of the students increases.)

Day 2: *Exercises*

Students complete the exercises and go through the notes/questions on the organization of the reading passage. If there is enough time, the exercises are checked orally.

Day 3: *Presentation of Model*

If the exercises were not checked before, they are checked now. Then, the model is presented by following some or all of the steps used in presenting the reading text on Day 1. Next, the teacher goes over the instructions for the students' compositions. Drawing boxes on the blackboard to represent paragraphs and labeling them as to their function and content is often helpful. The students' homework assignment for Day 4 is to mentally plan their compositions or plan them on paper in outline form. (The teacher may need to show students how to make an outline.)

Day 4: *Composition*

Students write their compositions in class. They should not copy the model, but exhaust the resources that it provides.

Day 5: *Wrap-up*

The class should finish any work that is left over from Days 1-4. If the teacher has checked all of the compositions, common problems should be explained. Orally or with an overhead projector, some compositions which illustrate points that the teacher wants to make might be shared with the class. The teacher may want students to rewrite their compositions, correcting and expanding.

Some composition classes in non-intensive programs may meet only two hours per week over a sixteen-week period. The students in such a program could take as long as two weeks to complete a unit and still cover most of the material in the book. The breakdown of each unit might then appear as follows:

Day 1 of the first week: *Reading*

The teacher presents the content of the reading according to the procedure outlined for Day 1 of the preceding five-day suggested plan for each unit. The students' homework for Day 2 is to do the exercises.

Day 2 of the first week: *Presentation of Model*

The exercises done for homework are checked orally. Then, the model is presented by following some or all of the steps used in presenting the reading text on Day 1. Next, the teacher goes over the instructions for the students' compositions. The students' homework assignment is to plan their compositions in outline form.

Day 1 of the second week on the unit: *Composition*

The teacher goes over the model again quickly in order to review and then the teacher checks students' outlines. Students then write their compositions in class.

Day 2 of the second week on the unit: *Wrap-up*

The teacher follows the procedure outlined for Day 5 of the preceding five-day plan for each unit.

Whatever the schedule, it is desirable that the actual writing of the compositions be done in class where the teacher is present to answer questions, make corrections, and offer suggestions. Students should be instructed to keep their compositions for future reference. At the end of the school term, the teacher can prepare a table of contents for a special composition notebook which each student will prepare, containing all the numbered and dated composition work for the term and including outlines, original drafts, and rewrites of each composition. This notebook can serve as a handy reference for future composition work.

After working through all the materials in this text, students should be able to write a one-page descriptive, narrative, or expository composition on a familiar, everyday subject, with an introduction, a body, and a conclusion, developed within the organizational framework of chronological order, classification, spatial order, shift of focus, ranking, or balance of contrasts.

To the student

You will need the following materials:

1. a loose-leaf notebook
2. 8½ x 11 loose-leaf notebook paper
3. a pen and pencil
4. a good translation dictionary and a simplified English-English dictionary

You should follow these rules for good reading:

1. Look at the complete reading selection before you use your dictionary. The meaning might become clear to you.
2. Let your eyes catch groups of words; do not stop after every word.
3. Do not move your mouth when you read; read with your eyes.
4. After you read the complete selection, use your dictionary to find the words that you do not know.
5. Read the selection again; look for important connections: *and, because, after, before, while,* etc.

You should follow these rules for good writing:

1. Leave margins: left, right, top, and bottom.
2. Indent each paragraph.
3. Put a period at the end of each sentence. Put a question mark at the end of each question. Put an exclamation mark if you want to show strong emotion.
   Examples: John is absent today.
   Is he sick?
   He had a terrible day!
4. Use capital letters correctly:
   a. names of people
      Example: John Andres
   b. names of cities
      Example: Paris
   c. names of countries
      Example: Japan
   d. names of rivers
      Example: the Amazon River
   e. names of streets
      Example: Michigan Avenue

f.   names of buildings
     Example: the Empire State Building
g.   names of organizations
     Example: the United Nations
h.   names of national, ethnic, and racial groups of people
     Example: French, Jewish, Negro
i.   titles
     Example: Dr. Santini
j.   the first person singular pronoun: *I*
k.   days of the week
     Example: Thursday
l.   months of the year
     Example: July
m.   holidays
     Example: Christmas
n.   titles of books, magazines, newspapers
     Example: Time
o.   the first letter at the beginning of each sentence and each question
     Example: Are you happy?

Placement of parts of a composition:

Your name
Course

Title

XXXXXXXXXXXXXXXXXXXXXXXXXXXXXXXXXXXXXXXX.
XXXXXXXXXXXXXXXXXXXXXXXXXXXXXXXX. XXXXXXXXXXX
XXXXXXXXXXXXXXXXXXXXXXXXXXXXXXXXXXXX. XXXXXXX
XXXXXXXXXXXXXXXXX. XXXXXXXXXXXXXXXXXXXXXXX
XXXXXXXXXXXXXXXXXXXXXXXXXXX.

XXXXXXXXXXXXXXXXXXXXXXXXXXXXX
XXXXXXXXX. XXXXXXXXXXXXXXXXXXXXXXXXXXXXXXXXX
XXXXXXXXXXXXXXXXXXXXXXXXXXXXXXXX. XXXXX
XXXXXXXXXXXXXXXXXXXXXXXXXXXXXXXXX
XXXXXXXXXXXXXXXXXXXXXXX. XXXXXXXXXXX
XXXXXXXXXXXXXXXXXXXXXXXXXXXX. XXXXXX
XXXXXXXXXXXXXX. XXXXXXXXXXXXXXXXXXX
XXXXXXXXXXXXXXXXXXXX.

XXXXXXXXXXXXXXXXXXXXXXXXXXXX.
XXXXXXXXXXXXXXXXXXXXXXXXXXXX. XXXXXXXXXX
XXXXXXXXXXXXXXXXXXXXXXXXXXXXXXXXXXXXXXXX
XXXXXXXXXXXXXXX. XXXXXXXXXXXXXXXXXXXXXXXXXXX
XXXXXXXXXX.

indentation

left margin   right margin

Unit 1

Grammatical Focus: Subject + Non-*be* (present tense)
Frequency words, e.g., *usually, always*

Composition Focus: Narration

Organizational Focus: Chronological order

Robert's Daily Activities

Robert lives in an apartment building. His apartment is on the twelfth floor. He lives in a two-bedroom apartment. He shares the apartment with a roommate. Robert pays half of the rent and his roommate pays the other half. Robert works every day. He is a cashier in a grocery store.

Robert gets up about 7:00 every morning. An alarm clock wakes him up. Robert wants to stay in shape, so he always does exercises for ten or fifteen minutes. Next, he goes to the bathroom to shower and shave. He gets dressed before he eats breakfast. For breakfast, he usually has coffee, toast, and fruit. He doesn't like to eat a big breakfast. After breakfast, he cleans up the kitchen. He likes to listen to the morning news on the radio while he does the dishes. By 8:15, he is ready to leave for work. He goes to work by train.

Robert arrives at work about 8:45. First, he takes off his coat and puts on a special jacket. The name of the grocery store is on the jacket. Then, he fills the drawer of the cash register with change. He stands behind the cash register all day. He eats a sandwich and drinks some tea when he has time. He finishes work at 4:30. Then, he takes the train back home.

In the evening, Robert and his roommate often prepare dinner together. They are both good cooks. They watch the six o'clock news on T.V. while they eat dinner. After that, they sometimes watch T.V., listen to the radio, or read. Both of them like to read. Robert usually goes to bed early because he is tired. He rarely stays up late.

In conclusion, Robert usually has a busy day. He works hard and does his job well.

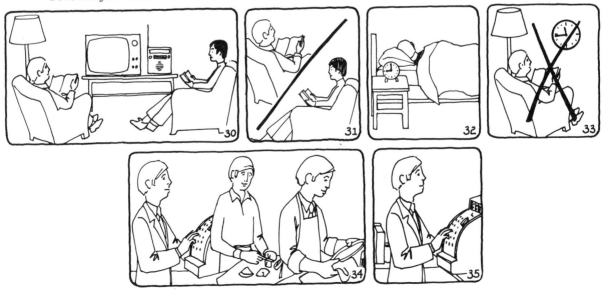

Please *circle* the letter to show the correct information. The information comes from Reading 1.

1. Robert lives on the
    a. tenth floor.
    b. eleventh floor.
    c. twelfth floor.

2. He lives
    a. with his mother.
    b. with a roommate.
    c. with his cousin.

3. He is
    a. a cashier.
    b. a clerk.
    c. a carpenter.

4. He does exercises because
    a. he is fat.
    b. he wants to stay in shape.
    c. he likes to play soccer.

5. He gets dressed
    a. before breakfast.
    b. during breakfast.
    c. after breakfast.

6. He goes to work
    a. by bus.
    b. on foot.
    c. by train.

7. He works
    a. in the produce section.
    b. at the cash register.
    c. behind the meat counter.

8. He often eats dinner
    a. with his roommate.
    b. with a friend.
    c. alone.

9. In the evening, Robert likes to
    a. drink beer.
    b. go dancing.
    c. read.

10. Robert goes to bed early because
    a. he is tired.
    b. he needs to get up early.
    c. he likes to sleep.

Please *list* ten of Robert's daily activities. *Use* the **simple present tense.** *Pay attention* to the 3rd-person singular verb form.

Example: *He gets up at 7:00.*
                He does exercises.
                etc.

1.

2.

3.

4.

5.

6.

7.

8.

9.

10.

Please *rewrite* "Robert's Daily Activities" (Reading 1). *Change* the title to "My Daily Activities." Be sure to *indent* at the beginning of each new paragraph. Be sure to *change* the verb form. Begin this way:

My Daily Activities

I live in an apartment building. My apartment is on the twelfth floor. I live in a two-bedroom apartment. I share the apartment with a roommate. etc. etc.

STUDENT'S NOTES

Please *rewrite* the following sentences. *Put* the ***frequency word*** in parentheses into the sentence. *Be careful* with the word order.

Example: Robert does exercises after he gets up. (always)
          Robert always does exercises after he gets up.

1. For breakfast, he has coffee and toast. (usually)

    _____

2. He leaves for work at 8:15. (always)

    _____

3. He goes to work by train. (sometimes)

    _____

4. He is on time. (always)

    _____

5. He drinks tea and eats a sandwich. (often)

    _____

6. He and his roommate prepare dinner together. (often)

    _____

7. They watch T.V., listen to the radio, or read. (sometimes)

    _____

8. Robert goes to bed early. (usually)

    _____

9. He stays up late. (rarely)

    _____

10. Robert has a busy day. (usually)

    _____

Notes and questions on the *organization* of Reading 1.

Part A: *Paragraphs*

Reading 1 has five paragraphs. They tell the story of Robert's daily life. *Go back* to Reading 1. *Be sure* that you *see* five paragraphs. The following questions will help you understand the *system of paragraphs* in Reading 1:

1. Where do you find information about the beginning of Robert's day? Which paragraph?
2. Where do you find information about Robert at work? Which paragraph?
3. Where do you find information about Robert's evening?
4. What information does the first paragraph give? Why is it there?
5. Look at the last paragraph. It is very short. What does *in conclusion* mean? Why is the last paragraph there?

Part B: *Order*

The word *order* refers to what is first, what is second, what is third, etc., in your composition. There should be a reason for what is first, what is second, etc. The following questions will help you understand the order of Reading 1:

1. How much time does the second paragraph cover?
2. How much time does the third paragraph cover?
3. How much time does the fourth paragraph cover?
4. Is 7:00 a.m. before or after 8:45 a.m.?
5. Is 6:00 p.m. before or after 4:30 p.m.?
6. Is the order in the second, third, and fourth paragraphs from early to late or from late to early?

Time order is called *chronological order.* It can go from late to early or from early to late. *Think* of different composition topics that might use time order.

Notice these **connecting words** in Reading 1:

next	then
after	in the <u>(part of day)</u>
by <u>(time)</u>	while
first	before
after that	when

All of these words have a time meaning. *Ask* your teacher for examples if you don't understand. Now, *go on* to Model 1.

Maria's Daily Activities

Maria lives in a small apartment. It is on the second floor of an old building. She lives with her cousin. Maria is a student at Roosevelt University. She is studying psychology. She works part-time as a clerk in a department store.

Maria gets up early every morning. She usually takes a shower and gets dressed before she has breakfast. She doesn't usually have much time for breakfast, so she only has a piece of toast and a cup of coffee. After breakfast, she quickly cleans up the kitchen. Then, she leaves for school. She always goes to school by bus.

Maria arrives at school about 8:30. First, she goes to the cafeteria to meet her friends and have another quick cup of coffee. Then, she goes to class. She is in class from 9:00 to 1:00. She has a ten-minute break at 10:00 and a half-hour break at 11:30. She has lunch during her long break. After class, Maria goes to work. She works in a busy department store downtown. She likes her work and she likes to talk to the customers. She works very hard. At 5:00, she finishes work. Then, she takes the bus back home. It takes her a half-hour to get home.

In the evening, Maria sometimes has dinner with her cousin. When her cousin works late, Maria eats alone. She likes to listen to the radio while she eats. After dinner, she does the dishes. Then, she studies. She usually goes to bed late because she has a lot of homework.

In summary, Maria is a very busy person. She works hard and studies hard. She has a good life.

Instructions for student's composition

1. Write a composition about your daily activities on 8½ x 11 loose-leaf notebook paper. Give your composition a title.

2. Write five paragraphs. Put the following information in your paragraphs:
    Paragraph 1 – Introduce yourself. Where do you live? What do you do?
    Paragraph 2 – Tell about your morning activities (before work or school).
    Paragraph 3 – Tell about the main part of your day.
    Paragraph 4 – Tell about your evening activities.
    Paragraph 5 – Conclude with several general points.
    Remember to leave margins and indent for each paragraph.

3. Take as many structures, ideas, and words from Model 1 as you can use in your composition.

4. Your composition should look like this:

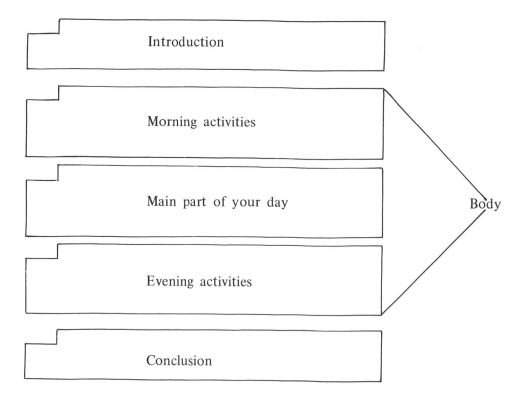

Unit 2

Grammatical Focus: Subject + Verb (present continuous tense)
                              Quantifiers, e.g., *most*, *all*, *several*

Composition Focus: Friendly letter in conversational tone, using description
                              and narration

Organizational Focus: Spatial order (1st paragraph)
                              Shift of conversational focus (the restaurant, I, you)

A Letter to a Friend

February 12, 1979

Dear Ernesto,

It is lunch time and I am sitting in a small restaurant close to my school. It is a cold day in Chicago. It is snowing and I am feeling homesick. I am thinking of you. Outside, the sidewalks are crowded with people. All of them are wearing heavy coats, boots, hats, and gloves. Everyone is in a hurry. Buses and cars are moving up and down the street. Inside, it is warm and pleasant. There are two pretty girls at the table next to mine. They are laughing and talking. In fact, I think one of the girls is smiling at me. Several students from my school are sitting at the counter. One of them is reading a newspaper while he is eating. An old man is sitting at a small table near the window. The waitress is serving him a piece of pie. It looks delicious.

I am fine. I am learning a lot in my classes. I like most of my teachers and classmates. I attend classes every afternoon, but I have plenty of time to study in the morning. I am having a good time in Chicago. There are a lot of things to see in this city, but I miss my friends and family.

I hope that you are well and happy. Please write soon. I enjoy your letters with news from home.

Your friend,

Roberto

Sample Envelope

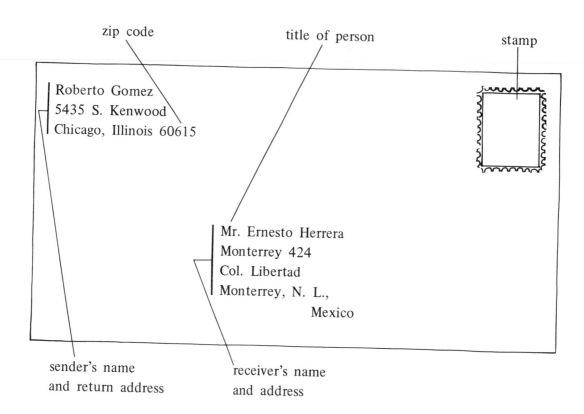

Note to the student:

There are different ways to conclude, or close, a letter:

Love (when you write to a special friend or relative)
Sincerely (when you write a business letter or write to a friend)
Your friend (when you write to a friend)
Your cousin (when you write to a cousin)

Your teacher can explain other possibilities.

Please *list* all verbs in Reading 2 that are in the ***present continuous tense***. *List* the infinitive and the present participle forms.

Example: *go*   *going*

1.

2.

3.

4.

5.

6.

7.

8.

9.

10.

11.

12.

13.

14.

Please *complete* the following sentences with **words of quantity.** *Find* each sentence in Reading 2 and *complete* it with the same words of quantity.

1. _____ are wearing heavy coats, boots, hats, and gloves.

2. _____ is in a hurry.

3. There are _____ pretty girls at the table next to mine.

4. In fact, I think _____ the girls is smiling at me.

5. _____ students from my school are sitting at the counter.

6. _____ is reading a newspaper while he is eating.

7. I am learning _____ in my classes.

8. I like _____ my teachers and classmates.

9. I attend classes _____ afternoon, but I have _____ _____ time to study in the morning.

10. There are _____ things to see in this city.

Please *reread* "A Letter to a Friend." *Underline* the **words for space.** Then, *complete* the sentences below with the words from the list below. Make these sentences the same as the sentences in Reading 2.

up and down	close to	at
in	near	outside
next to	inside	

1. I am sitting ＿＿＿＿＿＿＿＿＿ a small restaurant.

2. The restaurant is ＿＿＿＿＿＿＿＿＿ my school.

3. ＿＿＿＿＿＿＿＿＿ , the sidewalks are crowded with people.

4. Buses and cars are moving ＿＿＿＿＿＿＿＿＿ the street.

5. ＿＿＿＿＿＿＿＿＿ , it is warm and pleasant.

6. There are two pretty girls at the table ＿＿＿＿＿＿＿＿＿ mine.

7. Several students from my school are sitting ＿＿＿＿＿＿＿＿＿ the counter.

8. An old man is sitting at a small table ＿＿＿＿＿＿＿＿＿ the window.

STUDENT'S NOTES

Please *reorganize* the following groups of sentences. *Put* them into correct ***order***.
The order is according to ***space***. Most of the information is not from Reading 2.

1. There is a comfortable chair beside the table.
2. As you enter the room, you will see a large table.
3. In front of the chair, there is a small table.
4. On the small table, there is an ashtray.

    The correct order is ____ , ____ , ____ , ____ .

1. I am having lunch in the restaurant.
2. Next to my table, there are two pretty girls.
3. There is a restaurant near my school.
4. I am sitting near the window.

    The correct order is ____ , ____ , ____ , ____ .

1. In the back of the room, there are also windows.
2. Near the center of the room, there are many small desks.
3. I study in a pleasant classroom.
4. In the front of the room, there are large windows.

    The correct order is ____ , ____ , ____ , ____ .

1. Near the children, there is a small fountain.
2. There are trees and flowers around me.
3. Under the trees, children are playing.
4. I am sitting in a park.

    The correct order is ____ , ____ , ____ , ____ .

1. I am a waitress in a small restaurant.
2. It is warm and pleasant here.
3. People are walking in the snow.
4. Outside, it is snowing.

    The correct order is ____ , ____ , ____ , ____ .

Notes and questions on the *organization* of Reading 2:

Part A: *Paragraphs*

Reading 2 is a friendly letter. "Friendly" letter means that it is not a business letter. The form of a business letter is different. (See Unit 6.) Reading 2 has three paragraphs. *Go back* to Reading 2. *Be sure* that you *see* three paragraphs. *Notice* the date, the name of the receiver of the letter, and the name of the writer of the letter. The following questions will help you understand the *system of paragraphs* in Reading 2:

1. The first paragraph describes something. What does it describe? Why do you think that Roberto begins with a description? Will a description give Ernesto a "picture" of Roberto's daily life?
2. What information does the second paragraph give? Does it give more description? Who is the subject of the second paragraph?
3. What does the third paragraph do? Why is it last? Who is it about?

Is there really an *introduction*, a *body*, and a *conclusion* in a friendly letter? Is it the same as Reading 1 or Model 1? It isn't really, is it?

Part B: *Order*

Let's look at the first paragraph in Reading 2. The following questions will help you understand the *order* of the first paragraph. Remember that the word *order* refers to what is first, what is second, etc.

1. What is the place? Does Roberto begin with the details or with general information?
2. Does Roberto describe the outside or the inside first? Why?
3. Where does the description of the inside begin?
4. Does Roberto describe the furniture inside? The color of the walls? How does he describe the inside?
5. Where is everyone?

If the description tells "where," the writer is using *space order* or *spatial order. Think* of different descriptions that might need spatial order.

Notice these ***words for space*** in Reading 2:

in	inside
close to	at
outside	next to
up and down	near

Think of other words for space. *Ask* your teacher for help. Now, *go on* to Model 2.

A Letter to a Relative

July 1, 1979

Dear Elizabeth,

    It is Sunday afternoon and I am sitting on the beach. It is a warm summer day in Chicago. The sun is shining and I am thinking of you. The beach is crowded with people. Many of them are lying on the sand. To my left, some children are playing. To my right, three teenagers are laughing and talking. They are also listening to the radio. In front of me, an old man is reading a newspaper. Some people are walking up and down the beach. All of them seem happy to be outside. Several students from my school are sitting on the beach with me. In fact, I think you know one of them. His name is George and he is tall and thin. He says to tell you "Hello."

    I am fine. I am enjoying my classes. I am also learning a lot. I like all of my teachers. I attend classes five mornings a week, but I have time to study in the afternoon. I like Chicago but I miss you.

    How are you? I hope you are well and happy. When will you come for a visit? Please write soon. I always enjoy your letters.

Your cousin,

Barbara

Instructions for student's composition:

1. Write a letter to a friend or relative. Write on your own personal stationery, aerogramme, or a piece of 8½ x 11 loose-leaf notebook paper. Make it a real letter. Address the front of the aerogramme or an envelope to put the letter in.

2. Follow the form for a friendly letter. Write the date in the top right corner of your paper. To the left, 1½ inches down, write **Dear** _____ . Write three paragraphs. Put the following information in your paragraphs:

   Paragraph 1 — Describe where you are. What are you doing? What are other people doing?

   Paragraph 2 — Talk about your daily life.

   Paragraph 3 — Talk about the person you are writing to.

   Then, conclude the letter with **Sincerely** or some other appropriate conclusion. Then, write your first name.

3. Take what you need from Model 2. Let it help you with grammar, vocabulary, and ideas.

4. Your letter should look like this:

_____ (Date) _____

Dear _____ ,

Description of place

Talk about yourself

Talk about who you are writing to

Sincerely,
(Your name) _____

Unit 3

Grammatical Focus: Subject + *be* (simple present tense)
Future with *be going to*
Predicate adjectives

Composition Focus: Description

Organizational Focus: Classification (human characteristics: physical traits and personality traits)

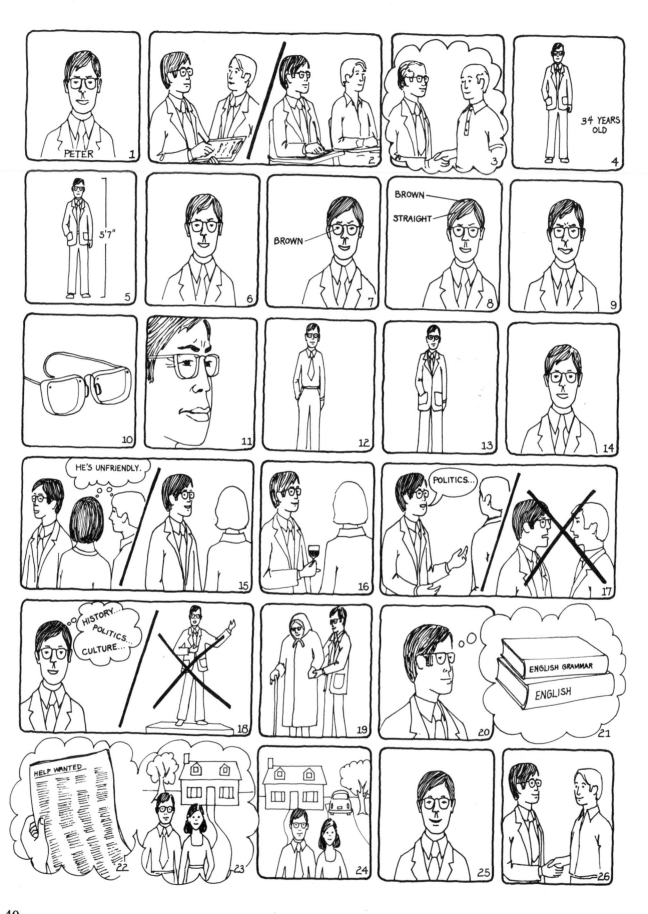

My Friend

Peter is one of my good friends. He is a friend from work and we are also classmates in evening school. I think that we are going to be long-time friends.

Peter is 34 years old. He is about 5 feet, 7 inches tall. His face is long and narrow. His eyes are brown. His hair is also brown and straight. He rarely smiles and usually has an unfriendly look on his face. He wears thick glasses. He doesn't smile very much because he doesn't see well. He is thin and has a slight build. He always wears a suit to work and to class.

Peter has a quiet personality. People think that he is unfriendly, but he really enjoys people. He likes to go to parties and have a good time. He likes to discuss politics, but he doesn't like to argue. He knows a lot, but he doesn't try to show off. Furthermore, he is kind and always tries to help.

Peter's future plans are very definite. First, he is going to improve his English. Then, he is going to look for another job. Next, he is going to buy a house and get married. In short, he is going to settle down. I am sure that he will be happy. He is a good person and a true friend.

Please *rewrite* the following sentences. *Use* ***is*** or ***are***. *Put* the adjective after the verb and *put* the noun before the verb. Use ***his*** at the beginning of each sentence.

Example: He has a long face.
           His face is long.

1. He has a narrow face.

   _____

2. He has brown eyes.

   _____

3. He has brown hair.

   _____

4. He has straight hair.

   _____

5. He has short hair.

   _____

6. He has a strange smile.

   _____

7. He has a quiet personality.

   _____

8. He has a slight build.

   _____

9. He has interesting ideas.

   _____

10. He has definite plans.

   _____

Exercise B: *Be going to*

Please *complete* the following. *Write* full sentences. Use **He is going to** at the beginning of each sentence. The time is **future**. You are writing about someone's future plans.

Example: return to his country
             He is going to return to his country.

1. become an engineer

     _____

2. improve his English

     _____

3. buy a house

     _____

4. look for another job

     _____

5. get married

     _____

6. go to evening school

     _____

7. get a college degree

     _____

8. settle down

     _____

9. study more English

     _____

10. take a trip

     _____

Please *complete* the following sentences. *Take* words from the list below. *Use* each one only one time. The words in the list **connect** the ideas of different parts of sentences or of different sentences.

in short	first	but
also	because	and
that	then	furthermore

1. I think _____ we are going to be long-time friends.

2. His face is long and narrow _____ his eyes are brown.

3. He is a friend from work and he is _____ a classmate.

4. He doesn't smile very much _____ he doesn't see well.

5. People think that he is unfriendly, _____ he really enjoys people.

6. He knows a lot, but he doesn't try to show off. _____ , he is kind and always tries to help.

7. Peter's plans are definite. _____ , he is going to improve his English. After that, he is going to buy a house.

8. He is going to improve his English. _____ , he is going to look for another job.

9. He is going to get a good job. Then, he is going to buy a house and get married. _____ , he is going to settle down.

Reading 3 is repeated below without *punctuation*. Please *read* through it and *add commas* and *periods*. The grammar and the capital letters will help you. *Go back* to Reading 3 and *check* your work after you finish.

My Friend

Peter is one of my good friends He is a friend from work and we are also classmates in evening school I think that we are going to be long-time friends

Peter is 34 years old He is about 5 feet 7 inches tall His face is long and narrow His eyes are brown His hair is also brown and straight He rarely smiles and usually has an unfriendly look on his face He wears thick glasses He doesn't smile very much because he doesn't see well He is thin and has a slight build He always wears a suit to work and to class

Peter has a quiet personality People think that he is unfriendly but he really enjoys people He likes to go to parties and have a good time He likes to discuss politics but he doesn't like to argue He knows a lot but he doesn't try to show off Furthermore he is kind and always tries to help

Peter's future plans are very definite First he is going to improve his English Then he is going to look for another job Next he is going to buy a house and get married In short he is going to settle down I am sure that he will be happy He is a good person and a true friend

STUDENT'S NOTES

Notes and questions on the *organization* of Reading 3.

Part A: *Paragraphs*

Reading 3 is a description of a person. There are four paragraphs. *Read* them again. *Notice* the differences in the content of the paragraphs. The following questions will help you understand the *system of paragraphs* in Reading 3:

1. Where do you begin to get details about Peter? Why is the first paragraph there, then? What does it do?
2. What kind of details do you get in the second paragraph?
3. What information does the third paragraph give you? How is it different from the second paragraph?
4. Does the fourth paragraph give you some new information? How does it serve as a conclusion?

A *conclusion* can repeat, summarize, emphasize, or add to the information in a composition. Sometimes, it does a little of everything.

Part B: *Order*

The following questions and comments will help you understand the order of Reading 3:

1. What is the general topic of Reading 3? It is true that "Peter" is the topic, but what is the more general topic?
2. That general topic is divided into two parts, or categories. What are they? (*Look* at the second and third paragraphs.)
3. *Look* at the second paragraph. Notice that the writer begins the physical description with the head and face (after giving age and height).
4. Is it possible to change the order of the two categories? Can personality come before physical appearance? Which order do you prefer?

A division of a general topic into sub-topics, or parts, or classes is called *classification*. *Think* of topics that you might classify. (There are many examples in science.) Next, *go on* to Model 3.

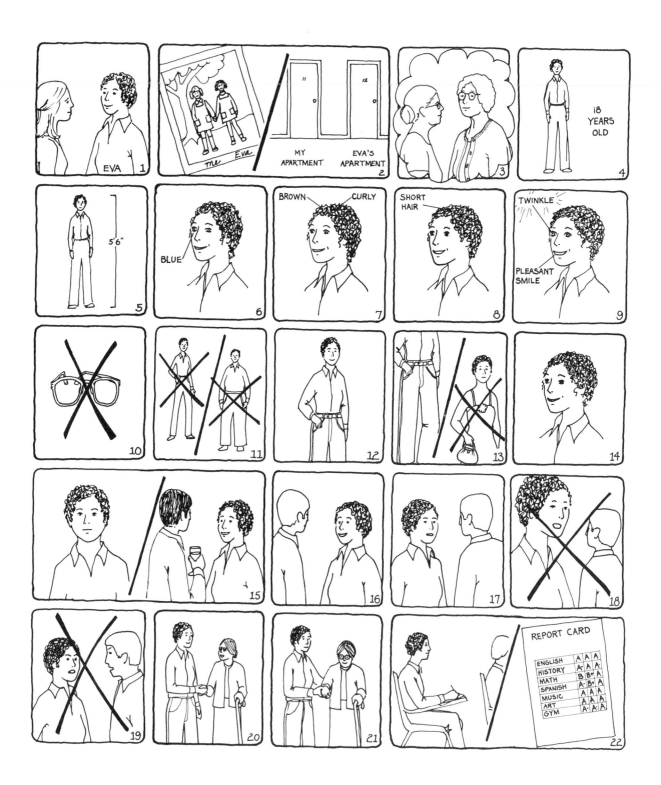

My Friend

Eva is a very good friend. She is a friend from elementary school and we are also neighbors. I think that we are going to be friends for a long, long time.

Eva is 18 years old. She is about 5 feet, 6 inches tall. Her eyes are blue and her face is round. Her hair is brown and very curly. She wears it short. She has a very pleasant smile and she always has a twinkle in her eye. She doesn't wear glasses. She isn't thin and she isn't fat. Her build is medium. She usually wears blue jeans and she doesn't like to get dressed up.

Eva has a wonderful personality. She is very serious, but she also likes to go to parties. She enjoys people. She likes to discuss serious subjects. She is very knowledgeable, but she doesn't like to make other people feel inferior. She doesn't like to argue. Furthermore, she is very polite and kind. She is always ready to help. Eva is a good student and always gets good grades.

Eva's future plans are a little uncertain. However, she thinks that she is going to study philosophy. Next year, she is going to attend the University of Illinois. She is going to live at home to save money. She is going to get a part-time job. In sum, I am sure that she will be successful. She is hard-working and intelligent.

Instructions for student's composition:

1. Write a composition about a friend on 8½ x 11 loose-leaf notebook paper. Describe your friend. Give your composition a title.

2. Write four paragraphs. Put the following information in your paragraphs:

    Paragraph 1 — Introduce your friend. How do you know him/her? What do you think of the friendship?

    Paragraph 2 — Describe your friend physically: age, color of hair, color of eyes, face, body, clothes, etc.

    Paragraph 3 — Describe your friend's personality.

    Paragraph 4 — Conclude with your friend's future plans. Give your feelings about your friend's future.

3. Take what you need from Model 3. Let it help you with grammar, vocabulary, and ideas.

4. Your composition should look like this:

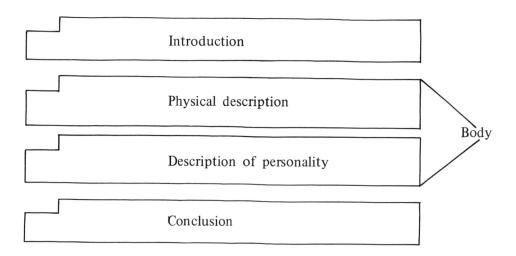

Unit 4

Grammatical Focus: Imperative
                    Modals: *can, should, will, might, may*

Composition Focus: Process description

Organizational Focus: Chronological order

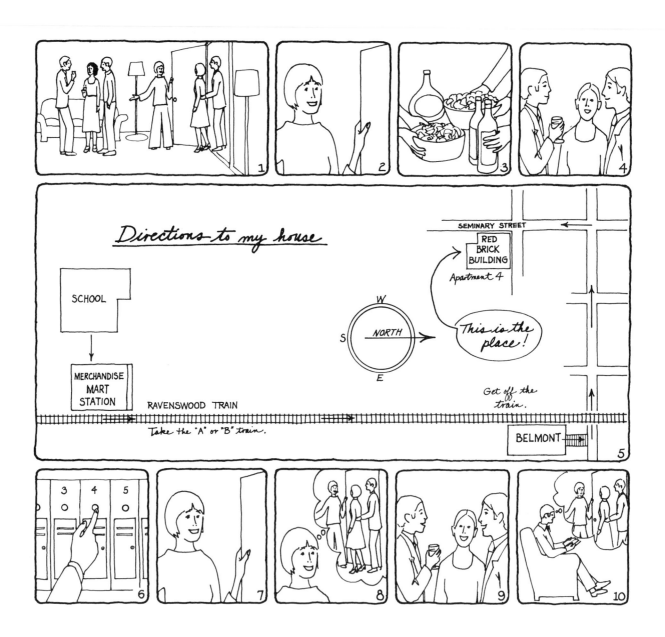

How to Get to My House

Some people like to give parties, but everyone likes to go to them. Giving a party can be fun. It can be easy and inexpensive, too, if all of the guests bring something to eat or drink. If you want to come to a good party next Saturday night, follow these directions to my house. The directions will lead you from school to my house by train. Please bring something to eat or drink.

First, you should walk over to the Merchandise Mart station and get on the Ravenswood train. You can take the "A" or "B" train. Take the train north to Belmont. It will take you about 15 minutes to get to Belmont. At Belmont, get off the train. Then, walk down the stairs to street level. Next, turn to your left and walk three blocks west. This will lead you to Seminary Street. You should turn left on Seminary and walk one block south. On the corner, you will see a red brick building with a large glass entrance. This is the place! Ring the bell for apartment 4 and I will let you in.

I hope that you will come to the party. You may also bring a friend. Come and enjoy yourself! You might miss a good time if you don't come.

Please *list* all of the **simple imperatives** (no subject, no auxiliary) in Reading 4.

Example: *Meet me there.*

1.

2.

3.

4.

5.

6.

7.

8.

9.

Rewrite each of the following sentences. Use the ***modal auxiliary*** in parentheses. After you finish, *check* your sentences with the same sentences in Reading 4.

1. Giving a party is fun. (can)

   _____

2. It is easy and inexpensive, too. (can)

   _____

3. The directions lead you from school to my house. (will)

   _____

4. First, you walk over to the Merchandise Mart station. (should)

   _____

5. You take the "A" or "B" train. (can)

   _____

6. It takes you about 15 minutes to get to Belmont. (will)

   _____

7. This leads you to Seminary Street. (will)

   _____

8. You turn left on Seminary and walk one block south. (should)

   _____

9. You also bring a friend. (may)

   _____

10. You miss a good time. (might)

    _____

The italicized part of each following sentence refers the reader to another part of the same sentence or to another sentence. All of the sentences come from Reading 4. What is the **reference**? Please *circle* the letter below the sentence to show the correct reference. *Find* each sentence in Reading 4 in order to decide.

1. Some people like to give parties, but everyone likes to go to *them.*

   What does *them* refer to?

   a.   some people

   b.   everyone

   c.   parties

2. *It* can be easy and inexpensive, too, if all of the guests bring something to eat or drink.

   What does *it* refer to?

   a.   giving a party

   b.   something to eat

   c.   something to drink

3. *This* will lead you to Seminary Street.

   What does *this* refer to?

   a.   getting off the train

   b.   walking down the stairs

   c.   turning left and walking west

4. This is *the place*!

   What does *the place* refer to?

   a.   Seminary Street

   b.   a red brick building with a large glass entrance

   c.   the fourth apartment

5. I hope you will come to *the party.*

   What does *the party* refer to?

   a.   a party that some people like to give

   b.   a party that everyone likes to go to

   c.   a party next Saturday night at my house

Please *reorganize* the following groups of sentences. Put them into correct *order.*
The order is according to *time* and *logic.*

1. First, walk over to the station.
2. Get off the train at Belmont.
3. Please follow these directions.
4. Then, get on the Ravenswood train.

                                         The correct order is ____ , ____ , ____ , ____ .

1. Next, walk three blocks west.
2. Turn left at the end of the third block.
3. Then, walk down the stairs to the street.
4. Get off the train at Belmont.

                                         The correct order is ____ , ____ , ____ , ____ .

1. Walking three blocks west will lead you to Seminary.
2. Now, you are in front of my house.
3. On Seminary Street, walk one block south.
4. Turn left on Seminary Street.

                                         The correct order is ____ , ____ , ____ , ____ .

1. Your friend doesn't need to bring anything to eat or drink.
2. I hope you will come to the party.
3. You may also bring a friend.
4. See you then!

                                         The correct order is ____ , ____ , ____ , ____ .

STUDENT'S NOTES

Notes and questions on the *organization* of Reading 4.

Part A: *Paragraphs*

Reading 4 describes how to do something. "How to" is a process. Therefore, Reading 4 is called a process description. There are three paragraphs. The following questions will help you understand the *system of paragraphs* in Reading 4:

1. Where does the process begin?
2. What does the first paragraph do, then? Where does the reader get the topic of the composition? How does the writer lead to the topic?
3. Where do the directions end? In other words, where does the process stop?
4. What does the last paragraph do?

The first paragraph usually introduces the topic, or subject, of the composition. Therefore, it is called the *introduction*. It leads the reader to the main part of the composition.

Part B: *Order*

Let's look at the second paragraph in Reading 4. The following questions and comments will help you understand the order:

1. Should the party-goer walk to the station before or after getting on the train?
2. Which is first—taking the train north or getting off the train?
3. Does the party-goer walk down the stairs before or after turning left?
4. The order is "time," isn't it? Is the time order first to last or last to first? *Notice* the time words in the second paragraph.
5. If the process is described in the second paragraph, is "time" necessary in the first and third paragraphs? Why not?

Process descriptions usually need *time order,* or *chronological order. Think* of other kinds of topics that might use chronological order. Now, *go on* to Model 4.

How to Make Spinach Pie

Some people like to cook, but everyone likes to eat. Cooking can be fun and it can be easy, too. If you want to make something that is quick, easy, and delicious, follow this recipe for spinach pie.

First, beat 2 eggs. Add 6 tablespoons of flour and continue to beat until the mixture is smooth. Then, add a 10-ounce package of frozen spinach. The spinach should be chopped. Stir the mixture. Next, add 1½ cups of cottage cheese, 1 cup of grated cheddar cheese, and ½ teaspoon of salt. Mix well. After that, grease the bottom and sides of a baking dish. Then, pour the mixture into the dish. Finally, cover the dish and put it in the oven. Bake the spinach pie for 1 hour at 350°. The pie will serve 4 people.

After you take the pie out of the oven, you will need to let it cool for a few minutes. Then, serve it with a fresh green salad, warm bread, and red wine. Fresh fruit might be nice for dessert. Enjoy your dinner!

Instructions for student's composition:

1. Write a composition on 8½ x 11 loose-leaf notebook paper. Tell someone how to do or make something. You might write out a recipe or tell someone how to build something. Give your composition a title.

2. Write three paragraphs. Put the following information in your paragraphs:

   Paragraph 1 — Introduce your idea. What are you talking about? Can people use it?

   Paragraph 2 — Describe the process. What comes first? What is second? What is next? etc.

   Paragraph 3 — What is the end of the process? Conclude with some general points.

   Be sure to leave margins and indent for each paragraph.

3. Take what you need from Model 4. Let it help you with grammar, vocabulary, and ideas.

4. Your composition should look like this:

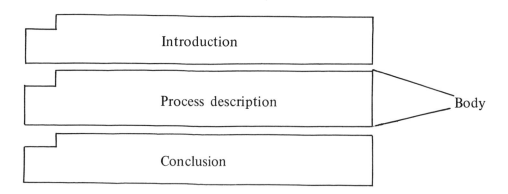

Unit 5

Grammatical Focus: Subject + Verb (simple past tense; regular and irregular verbs)
Objects: direct and indirect

Composition Focus: Narration

Organizational Focus: Chronological order

Yesterday

Yesterday was a typical school day for me. It was long, but it was interesting. In the morning, I went to class and spent some time in the library. In the afternoon, I went to work. In the evening, I relaxed a little and studied some more. That is the way my life goes.

My alarm clock rang at 7:00. I jumped out of bed and did some exercises. Then, I took a quick, cold shower. While I was in the bathroom, I shaved, brushed my teeth, and combed my hair. I also put on some after-shave lotion. At this point, I was ready to face the day! After I got dressed, I went to the kitchen to fix a big breakfast of scrambled eggs, bacon, toast, and coffee. At 8:00, I put on my coat and left for school.

Yesterday, the expressway was unusually crowded, so it took me almost an hour to drive to school. I parked in the lot next to the college. Then, I ran upstairs for a quick cup of coffee before class. By 9:00, I was in class. In one of the classes, the teacher taught us some new technical terms and explained an engineering problem to us. I attended three classes in a row with only a ten-minute break between classes. After class, I went to the library. There, I did my homework for the next day and looked up some information for a research project. I also asked the librarian some questions about engineering books. Afterwards, I bought lunch for myself and a friend in the school cafeteria.

The rest of the day passed as usual. I worked until 5:00 in the Merchandise Mart across the river from the college. I work in a newsstand there. I sold a lot of newspapers and magazines to my regular customers. I got home about 5:45, had dinner, and then collapsed in front of the T.V. for a while. Then, I studied for a couple of hours. By that time, it was midnight and I fell into bed.

Part 1: Please *reread* Reading 5. *Look* for verbs in the ***simple past tense.*** *List* them below. List the verb and its past tense form. (There are 29 different verbs in the simple past tense; list each verb only one time.)

Example: *go*   *went*

1.   16.

2.   17.

3.   18.

4.   19.

5.   20.

6.   21.

7.   22.

8.   23.

9.   24.

10.   25.

11.   26.

12.   27.

13.   28.

14.   29.

15.

Part 2: Please *change* these sentences to the ***past***. *Change* the verb to the simple past tense. If there is a present time word, *change* it to a past time word.

Example: Every morning, I go to class.
          Yesterday morning, I went to class.

1. Every morning, I go to work.

    _____

2. Every evening, I relax a little and study some.

    _____

3. My alarm clock rings at 7:00 every morning.

    _____

4. Every morning, I do some exercises.

    _____

5. While I am in the bathroom, I shave, brush my teeth, and comb my hair.

    _____

6. After I get dressed, I go to the kitchen to fix breakfast.

    _____

7. The expressway is crowded, so it takes me an hour to drive to school.

    _____

8. I run upstairs for a quick cup of coffee before class.

    _____

9. By 9:00 every morning, I am in class.

    _____

10. I attend three classes in a row every day.

    _____

11. I do my homework for the next day.

    _____

12. I work until 5:00 every afternoon.

    _____

13. I get home about 5:45, have dinner, and collapse in front of the T.V.

    _____

14. By this time, it is midnight and I fall into bed.

    _____

Exercise B: Objects

Pretend that you are the person who wrote Reading 5; in other words, you are "I." Please *answer* the following questions with information from Reading 5. *Pay attention* to the position of the **objects**.

1. What did you do after you jumped out of bed?

   _____

2. What did you do after you did some exercises?

   _____

3. Why did you go to the kitchen?

   _____

4. How long did it take you to get to school?

   _____

5. What did the teacher do in one of the classes?

   _____

6. What did you do in the library? (List three activities.)

_____

_____

_____

7. What did you do after you left the library?

_____

8. What did you do at the newsstand?

_____

9. What did you do after you got home?

_____

Exercise C: Chronological Order

Please *reorganize* the following sentences. *Put* them into correct ***time order.***
(Another name for time order is ***chronological order.*** It is the same.)

1. In the afternoon, I went to work.
2. That is the way my life goes.
3. In the evening, I relaxed a little.
4. In the morning, I went to class.

The correct order is _____ , _____ , _____ , _____ .

1. After I jumped out of bed, I did some exercises.
2. After my shower, I got dressed.
3. My alarm clock rang at 7:00.
4. Next, I took a shower.

The correct order is _____ , _____ , _____ , _____ .

1. I left for school at 8:00.
2. By 9:00, I was in class.
3. After class, I went to the library.
4. It took me almost an hour to get to school.

    The correct order is ____ , ____ , ____ , ____ .

1. Then, it took me forty-five minutes to drive home.
2. I worked until 5:00 in the newsstand.
3. Before I left the newsstand, I said goodbye to my boss.
4. After I got home, I had dinner and watched T.V.

    The correct order is ____ , ____ , ____ , ____ .

1. By 10:30, I was ready for bed.
2. After dinner, I read for a while and wrote some letters.
3. I watched the news on T.V. while I ate.
4. I had dinner around 6:00.

    The correct order is ____ , ____ , ____ , ____ .

Exercise D: Capitalization

Reading 5 is repeated below without *capital letters*. Please *read* through it and *add* capital letters. The grammar and the punctuation will help you. *Go back* to Reading 5 and *check* your work after you finish.

yesterday

yesterday was a typical school day for me. it was long, but it was interesting. in the morning, i went to class and spent some time in the library. in the afternoon, i went to work. in the evening, i relaxed a little and studied some more. that is the way my life goes.

my alarm clock rang at 7:00. i jumped out of bed and did some exercises. then, i took a quick, cold shower. while i was in the bathroom, i shaved, brushed my teeth, and combed my hair. i also put on some after-shave lotion. at this point, i was ready to face the day! after i got dressed, i went to the kitchen to fix a big breakfast of scrambled eggs, bacon, toast, and coffee. at 8:00, i put on my coat and left for school.

yesterday, the expressway was unusually crowded, so it took me almost an hour to drive to school. i parked in the lot next to the college. then, i ran upstairs for a quick cup of coffee before class. by 9:00, i was in class. in one of the classes, the teacher taught us some new technical terms and explained an engineering problem to us. i attended three classes in a row with only a ten-minute break between classes. after class, i went to the library. there, i did my homework for the next day and looked up some information for a research project. i also asked the librarian some questions about engineering books. afterwards, i bought lunch for myself and a friend in the school cafeteria.

the rest of the day passed as usual. i worked until 5:00 in the merchandise mart across the river from the college. i work in a newsstand there. i sold a lot of newspapers and magazines to my regular customers. i got home about 5:45, had dinner, and then collapsed in front of the t.v. for a while. then, i studied for a couple of hours. by that time, it was midnight and i fell into bed.

Notes and questions on the *organization* of Reading 5.

Part A: *Paragraphs*

Reading 5 tells a kind of story. It is the story of someone's daily life. The writer explains the daily life by explaining a typical day in the past. There are four paragraphs. You might expect five paragraphs: an introduction, "morning," "afternoon," "evening," and a conclusion. *Look* carefully to understand the organization of Reading 5. *Look to see* how it is divided into paragraphs. The following questions will help you understand the *system of paragraphs* in Reading 5:

1. In the first paragraph, how does the writer divide the day?
2. Is the second paragraph about the morning?

3. What is the third paragraph about?
4. Where do you get information on the afternoon? On the evening?
5. How, then, is the day really divided?
6. How is the conclusion different from the other readings? The conclusion of the day is the conclusion of the composition, isn't it?

Sometimes, the **conclusion** of a composition is the end of the main part, or **body**. In Reading 5, the last part of the body is also the conclusion.

Part B: *Order*

By now, you probably already understand the order of Reading 5. The following questions will help you be sure:

1. How much time does the second paragraph cover?
2. How much time does the third paragraph cover? Is the time before or after the time in the second paragraph?
3. How much time does the last paragraph cover? Is the time before or after the time in the third paragraph?
4. *Look* for time words. Is the order from early to late or from late to early?

Remember that this kind of order is called **time order,** or **chronological order.** It is almost automatic to use time order in a composition on daily activities. Now, *go on* to Model 5.

Model 5

Yesterday

Yesterday was not a typical day for me. It was difficult and frustrating. In the morning, I was late for work. In the afternoon, I had a terrible examination. By evening, I was exhausted. I am glad that most days are different!

Something was wrong with my alarm clock and it did not ring at 6:45 as usual. As a result, I overslept. When I woke up, it was 7:30. I jumped out of bed, threw on my clothes, and ran to catch the bus. Poor me! I didn't have time for one little cup of coffee.

I arrived at work a half-hour late. When I opened the door, my boss gave me a dirty look. Before I had time to give him my excuse, he told me his opinion about lazy employees. I felt terrible! Finally, he listened to me while I explained my problem to him. He told me to buy myself a new alarm clock. That made me angry.

The rest of the day was also bad. When I got to school, I borrowed some class notes from a friend and he helped me study a little for the examination. He explained some scientific terms to me. After I studied his notes, I was more unhappy. I didn't understand anything! At 2:00, I hurried to the classroom. I didn't want to be late for the exam. I took the exam, but I don't think I passed it. It was very difficult and the teacher didn't give us any help. I felt sick! I went home after the exam and collapsed in front of the T.V. I told my sister my sad story. Then, we had dinner and talked for a while. By that time, it was 11:00 and I fell into bed. What a day!

Instructions for student's composition:

1. Write a composition about *yesterday* on 8½ x 11 loose-leaf notebook paper. Describe your day.

2. Write four paragraphs. Don't forget to leave margins and indent for each paragraph. Put the following information in your paragraphs:

   Paragraph 1 — What kind of day was yesterday? What was your main morning activity? What was your main afternoon activity? What was your main evening activity? How did you feel by evening?

   Paragraph 2 — Describe your morning (early).

   Paragraph 3 — Describe the main part of your day.

   Paragraph 4 — Describe the rest of your day. Conclude with bedtime.

3. Use as much of Model 5 as you need. Let it help you with grammar, vocabulary, and ideas.

4. Your composition should look like this:

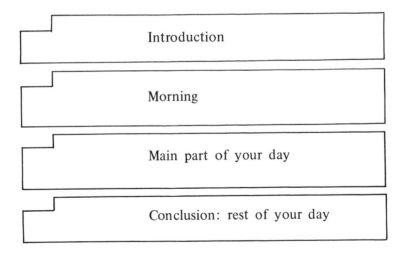

Introduction

Morning

Main part of your day

Conclusion: rest of your day

STUDENT'S NOTES

Unit 6

Grammatical Focus: Imperative
                          Polite request with *would*

Composition Focus: Business letter

Organizational Focus: Ranking of requests

A Business Letter

9873 S. Damen
Chicago, Illinois 60643
February 3, 1979

Ms. Mary Lima
Personnel Director
Lexington Steel Corporation
5543 S. Western Avenue
Chicago, Illinois 60617

Dear Ms. Lima:

I would like to request an interview for the position of typist. I saw your advertisement in Sunday's *Chicago Tribune.* I can type at 80 words per minute. I can take shorthand at 120 words per minute. I have a diploma from a secretarial school in Germany. I worked for five years as a typist in the Admissions Office at the University of Heidelberg. I arrived in the United States eight months ago. Now, I am studying English at Loop College. My English is good and my secretarial skills are excellent.

I would like to work for Lexington Steel Corporation. I would be happy to give you a list of references and a complete resumé of my work experience.

Please contact me at the above address. Thank you very much.

Sincerely,

Hilda Eckman

Hilda Eckman

Please *reread* Reading 6. Then, *answer* the following questions. They test your **comprehension,** or your **understanding** of Reading 6. *Go back* to Reading 6 if you have trouble.

1. Where does Hilda Eckman live?
   a. 5543 S. Western
   b. 9873 S. Damen
   c. Heidelberg, Germany
   d. Loop College

2. When did Hilda Eckman write the letter?
   a. Sunday
   b. Five years ago
   c. Eight months ago
   d. February 3, 1979

3. What is the zip code for Lexington Steel Corporation?
   a. 60643
   b. 5543
   c. 60617
   d. 80120

4. Why did Hilda Eckman write to Mary Lima to request a job interview?
   a. Because Ms. Lima works for the *Chicago Tribune.*
   b. Because Ms. Lima is a typist.
   c. Because Ms. Lima is the personnel director.
   d. Because Ms. Lima teaches at Loop College.

5. What are Hilda Eckman's secretarial skills?
   a. She can type and take shorthand.
   b. She can speak English.
   c. She has a secretarial diploma.
   d. She has experience as a typist.

6. What is Hilda Eckman's work experience?

    a.   She worked for eight months in the United States.

    b.   She has a diploma from a secretarial school.

    c.   She has a diploma from Loop College.

    d.   She worked as a typist in Heidelberg for five years.

7. Where does Hilda Eckman want to receive an answer to her letter?

    a.   5543 S. Western

    b.   9873 S. Damen

    c.   the University of Heidelberg

    d.   Loop College

STUDENT'S NOTES

Please *rewrite* the following sentences. *Change* **want to** to **would like to**. **Would like to** is more polite; it means **allow me** or **permit me** when you direct it to someone. It is an ***indirect request***.

Example: I want to request an interview.
               I would like to request an interview.

1. I want to apply for a job.

   _____

2. I want to receive an application.

   _____

3. I want to get a diploma from the Secretarial Institute.

   _____

4. I want to work in the Admissions Office.

   _____

5. I want to study English at Loop College.

   _____

6. I want to work for Lexington Steel Corporation.

   _____

7. I want to be a typist in your office.

   _____

8. I want to show you my references.

   _____

9. I want to send you a resumé of my work experience.

   _____

10. I want to thank you.

    _____

Please *write* one request for each of the following situations. *Use* the **imperative** with **please.** *Use* **me, to me,** or **for me** in each request. *Use* the verb in parentheses.

Example: You have a question. You need an answer. (answer)
             Please answer a question for me.

1. You need an application form. (send)

    _____

2. You need some information. (give)

    _____

3. You want to know the rules. (explain)

    _____

4. You need a college catalog. (send)

    _____

5. You want to receive a phone call or letter. (contact)

    _____

6. You want to receive a letter at your home address. (write)

    _____

7. You want to know the schedule. (tell)

    _____

8. You know the answer. You want someone to ask a question. (ask)

    _____

9. You want to understand the problem. (explain)

    _____

10. You want to hear the news. (tell)

    _____

Please *rewrite* each request from Exercise C. *Use* **Would you please** to make a polite ***direct request.***

Example: You have a question. You need an answer. (answer)
Please answer a question for me. (Exercise C)
Would you please answer a question for me?

1.

2.

3.

4.

5.

6.

7.

8.

9.

10.

Notes and questions on the *organization* of Reading 6.

Part A: *Paragraphs*

Reading 6 is a business letter. *Notice* that the form is a little different from the friendly letter in Unit 2. *Look* at the differences. There are three paragraphs in Reading 6, in addition to the other parts (addresses, names, etc.). The following questions will help you understand Reading 6. The *system of paragraphs* in a business letter is different from a regular composition.

1. Does the first paragraph lead the reader to the main part in the second paragraph? If not, what does it do?
2. Is the second paragraph the main part, or body? If not, what is it? What does the reader get in the second paragraph?
3. What does the last paragraph do? What is last in the last paragraph?

A letter is different from a composition. A letter has a kind of *conclusion*, but the *introduction* and *body* are not the same. There is no separate introduction. The writer begins the letter with the main point.

Part B: *Order*

The following questions will help you understand the *order of information* in Reading 6:

1. What does the writer request in the first paragraph? Why is the other information there?
2. What is the second paragraph about? How does that information connect to the first paragraph? What is the point of the second paragraph?
3. What does the writer request in the third paragraph?
4. Of the three paragraphs, which contains the most central point? How important are the other points, or requests?

Think of other kinds of writing where you might *rank* information. *Ranking* means to put something first, then second, then third, etc. Writers often rank statistical information, such as populations of cities. How is ranking different from time order? *Ask* your teacher to explain. What might be a reason for ranking? With cities, for example, which one might go first? How do you decide? Now, *go on* to Model 6.

A Business Letter

5639 S. Blackstone
Chicago, Illinois 60615
January 14, 1979

Foreign Student Admissions Office
Northwestern University
633 Clark Street
Evanston, Illinois 60545

Dear Madam/Sir:

Please send me a catalog and an application for admission to the School of Engineering at Northwestern University. I have a diploma from a high school in Beirut, Lebanon. I arrived in the United States six months ago. Now, I am studying English at Loyola University. I would like to begin my studies at Northwestern in September, 1979. My major field of interest is mechanical engineering.

I would also like to receive information on tuition and housing. Would it be possible to live with an American family? In addition, I would also like to know about any scholarships for foreign students.

Would you please send all of this information as soon as possible? Please send it to the above address. Thank you very much.

Sincerely yours,

Ali Sharif

Ali Sharif

Instructions for student's composition:

1. Write a business letter to a company or an institution. Write on 8½ x 11 plain white paper or loose-leaf notebook paper. Make it look like a real letter. Address an envelope for the letter.

2. Follow the form for a business letter. Write your address and the date in the top right corner. To the left, 2 inches down, write the name and address of the person who will receive the letter. Under that, ¼ inch down, write *Dear Madam, Dear Sir,* or *Dear* (full name).

3. Write three paragraphs. Put the following information in your paragraphs:

    Paragraph 1 — What do you want? Tell about yourself (if appropriate).
    Paragraph 2 — Add any other requests or information.
    Paragraph 3 — When do you want an answer? Where do you want to receive an answer? Say thank you.
    Then, conclude with *Sincerely* or *Sincerely yours.* Sign your full name.

4. Take what you need from Model 6. Let it help you with the form of your letter, grammar, vocabulary, and ideas.

5. Your letter should look like this:

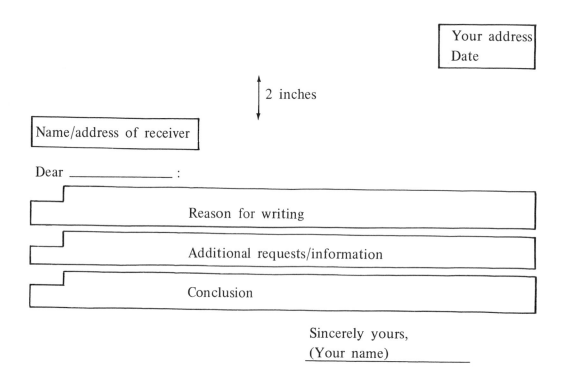

Unit

Grammatical Focus: Subject + Verb (simple past tense; regular and
irregular verbs)
Predicate infinitive (*to + verb*)

Composition Focus: Narration

Organizational Focus: Chronological order

A Terrible Trip

My brother and I took a trip to Miami last summer. I will never forget it. My grandmother and grandfather lived in Miami and they wanted us to come to visit them. We thought about the beaches and the wonderful climate, so we decided to go. We also wanted to see our grandparents.

We had a reservation on an early flight to Miami, so we got up before the sun rose. We were all excited about the trip. A friend came to drive us to the airport. That is where our problems started. On our way to the airport, we had a flat tire. This made us miss our flight. Then, we had to wait for three hours for another one. Because we were three hours late, our grandparents were not at the airport to meet us. We called their house and asked them to come back to the airport. We waited outside and my grandfather honked the horn as he drove up. We ran to greet him. Of course, we hugged and kissed him.

We stayed for two weeks and had a terrible time. On the second day, my grandmother fell and broke her arm. On the fifth day, I drove my grandfather's car into a tree. In addition, the weather was awful. It rained almost every day and the sun didn't shine. We didn't go to the beach one time.

When it was time to leave, we were both sad and happy. We wanted to return home, but we hated to leave our grandparents. We said goodbye and begged them to visit us in Chicago. Then, we got into a taxi to go to the airport. Guess what happened? Yes, the taxi broke down on the way to the airport. Someone stopped to help and drove us to the airport. We arrived just in time to catch our plane. When we arrived home, we were very tired, but we were happy to see Chicago. We agreed that it was a terrible trip.

Please *reread* Reading 7. *Look* for verbs in the ***simple past tense***. *List* them below. List the verb and its past tense form. (There are 33 different verbs; list each verb only once.)

Example: see   saw

1.   18.

2.   19.

3.   20.

4.   21.

5.   22.

6.   23.

7.   24.

8.   25.

9.   26.

10.   27.

11.   28.

12.   29.

13.   30.

14.   31.

15.   32.

16.   33.

17.

Please *change* these sentences to the ***past***. *Change* the verb to the ***simple past tense***. *Change* the present time word to a past time word.

Example: My brother and I take a trip to Miami every year.
                My brother and I took a trip to Miami last year.

1. My grandparents live in Miami all the time.

    _____

2. They want us to come to visit them every summer.

    _____

3. We think about the beaches all the time.

    _____

4. We get up before the sun rises every morning.

    _____

5. We are all excited about our trip today.

    _____

6. We have a flat tire once in a while.

    _____

7. My grandfather always honks the horn as he drives up.

    _____

8. We sometimes run out to greet him.

    _____

9. We always hug and kiss him.

    _____

10. Every summer, we stay for two weeks.

    _____

11. The weather is sometimes awful.

_____

12. It rains almost every Saturday.

_____

13. The sun doesn't always shine.

_____

14. We don't go to the beach every day.

_____

15. We say goodbye to our grandparents every weekend.

_____

Combine each group below. *Write* only one sentence for each group. Every verb after the first one should be in the *infinitive form* with **to**.

Example: They wanted us.
We came.
We visited them.
They wanted us to come to visit them.

1. We decided. We went.

    _____

2. We wanted. We saw our grandparents.

    _____

3. A friend came. A friend drove us to the airport.

    _____

4. Our grandparents were not at the airport. Our grandparents didn't meet us.

    _____

5. We called their house. We asked them. They came back to the airport.

    _____

6. We ran. We greeted him.

    _____

7. It was time. We left.

    _____

8. We hated. We left our grandparents.

    _____

9. We got into a taxi. We went to the airport.

    _____

10. Someone stopped. Someone helped.

    _____

11. We arrived just in time. We caught our plane.

    _____

Please *reread* Reading 5. *Look* for **words that connect** a subject and verb to another subject and verb. (Sometimes the second subject is not repeated.) *Underline* the connecting words: *and, so, because, as, when, but.* Next, *combine* each of the following groups of sentences. *Use* the connecting words in parentheses. Be careful with word order, punctuation, and capital letters.

Please *combine* these groups. *Write* a total of eight sentences.

1. My grandfather and grandmother lived in Miami.   (and)
   They wanted us to come to visit them.

   _____

2. We thought about the beaches and the wonderful climate.   (so)
   We decided to go.

   _____

3. We had a reservation on an early flight to Miami.   (so)
   We got up.   (before)
   The sun rose.

   _____

4. We were three hours late.   (because)
   Our grandparents were not at the airport to meet us.

   _____

5. We waited outside.   (and)
   My grandfather honked the horn.   (as)
   He drove up.

   _____

6. It was time to leave.   (when)
   We were both sad and happy.

   _____

7. We wanted to return home.   (but)
    We hated to leave our grandparents.

    _____

8. We arrived home.   (when)
    We were very tired.   (but)
    We were happy to see Chicago.

    _____

STUDENT'S NOTES

Notes and questions on the *organization* of Reading 7.

Part A: *Paragraphs*

Reading 7 tells the story of someone's trip. By now, you already know what basic *system of paragraphs* to expect. The following questions will guide you:

1. In which paragraph does the trip begin? What information comes before that point? What is the name for the paragraph leading to the main point?

2. In which paragraph does the trip end? How many paragraphs long is the body, then?

3. Is there a separate conclusion? There isn't, is there?

The system of paragraphs in Reading 7 is the same as in Reading 5. The end of the trip (in Reading 5, the end of the day) is the end of the composition. In other words, the last part of the *body* is the *conclusion.* This often happens when we write about a period of time.

Part B: *Order*

By now, you probably don't need questions to help you see when the *order of information* is *chronological. Check* the time words in Reading 7. *Look* again to see how the time is divided. In other words, where in the composition do you get the arrival and the departure? Where do you find information about the time in between? Now, *go on* to Model 7. *See* if it is organized the same way.

A Memorable Trip

I took a wonderful trip with my family when I was 10 years old. I remember it well. My aunt, uncle, and two cousins lived on a farm in Michigan and they invited us to visit them.

It was Saturday morning when we left home. We got up early that morning before the sun rose. We were all excited about the trip and ate breakfast quickly. We left home at 6:00 in order to get an early start. It took us five hours to get there. When we drove up to the house, my father honked the horn to announce our arrival. Everyone ran out to greet us. I hugged and kissed my aunt, uncle, and cousins.

We stayed for two days and had a wonderful time. We played in the barn and helped Uncle John feed and water the animals. He let us ride the horses and showed us how to pick apples. He also taught us how to play checkers. At night, we played checkers with our cousins and listened to the grown-ups tell stories.

When it was time to leave, we were very sad. They asked us to stay longer, but we had to go back home. My father had to go to work the next day. We said goodbye and asked our relatives to come and visit us. Then, we got into the car for the trip home. When we arrived home, we were tired and sleepy, but we were happy. We all agreed that it was a memorable trip.

Instructions for student's composition:

1. Write about a trip on 8½ x 11 loose-leaf notebook paper. Give details of the trip. Perhaps the trip was good; perhaps it was bad.

2. Write four paragraphs. Be sure to leave margins and indent for each paragraph. Put the following information in your paragraphs:

    Paragraph 1 — Where did you go? When did you go? Why did you go?
    Paragraph 2 — Tell about the beginning of the trip.
    Paragraph 3 — How long did you stay? What did you do?
    Paragraph 4 — Tell about coming home. Tell about your feelings.

3. Use as much of Model 7 as you need. Let it help you with grammar, vocabulary, ideas, and organization.

4. Your composition should look like this:

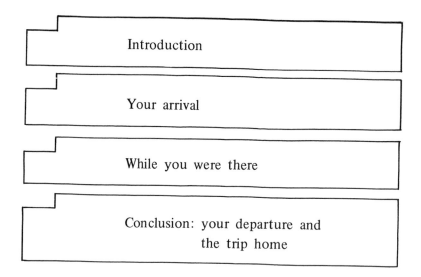

Introduction

Your arrival

While you were there

Conclusion: your departure and
the trip home

Unit

Grammatical Focus: Subject + Verb (simple present tense)

                                Expressions for weather

Composition Focus: Exposition

Organizational Focus: Classification (weather: seasons of the year)

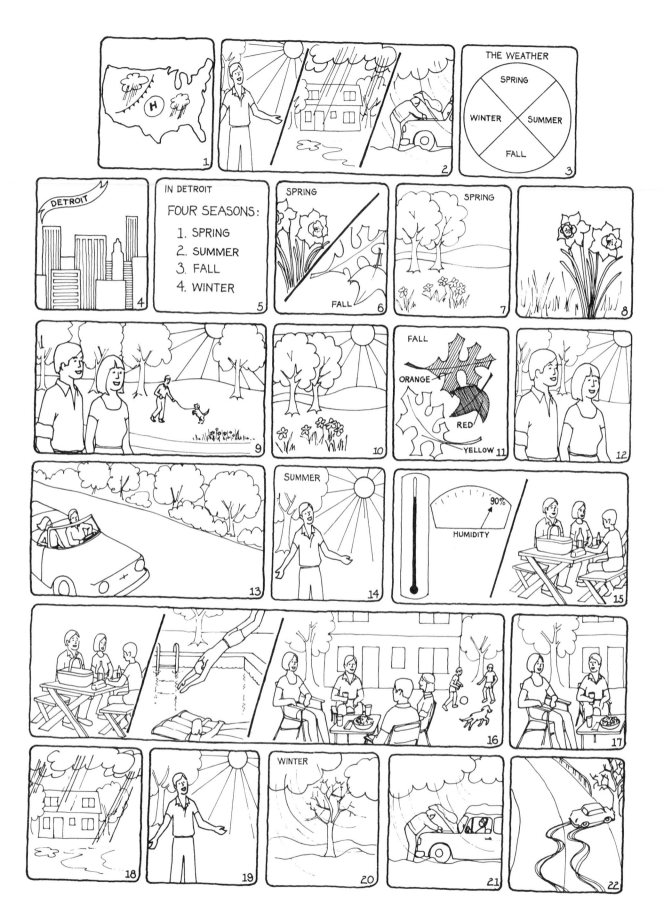

The Weather in Detroit

The weather is always very important to everyone. People's lives change with the weather. People usually divide the weather into seasons. I live in Detroit. In this part of the United States, there are four seasons: spring, summer, fall, and winter.

Spring and fall are lovely seasons. In the springtime, everything comes alive. The grass turns green and flowers begin to bloom. People seem happy and spend more time outside. The sun shines almost every day. In the fall, the leaves turn orange, yellow, and red. The weather is still warm and pleasant. People drive to the country in order to see the fall colors.

Summertime is wonderful. It gets very hot and humid, but I and my family have fun together. We go on picnics, go swimming, and have parties outside in the yard. We relax and take life easy. It sometimes rains, but that is not a problem. After the rain is over, the air is cool and pleasant.

Winter is the unpleasant season. It snows a lot and people have trouble with their cars. It is hard to drive and there are many accidents. Schools sometimes have to close because students can't get to school. People stay inside a lot. When they go outside, they need to wear heavy coats, boots, hats, and gloves. It gets very, very cold. The temperature sometimes drops to $0°$ Fahrenheit. I do not like winter!

In conclusion, life changes with the weather. In Detroit, there are four seasons and there are different activities for each season. I don't like for every day to be the same, but why can't two of the seasons be summer? Then, we could forget winter!

Please *complete* the following sentences. They tell about people in the summer and winter. *Use* the **simple present tense**. *Begin* each sentence with **In the . . . time, everyone . . .** Be careful with the 3rd-person singular verb form.

Part 1: *Summertime*

Example: go to the beach
         In the summertime, everyone goes to the beach.

  1. go swimming

  _____

  2. spend a lot of time outside

  _____

  3. lie in the sun

  _____

  4. go on picnics

  _____

  5. have parties outside

  _____

  6. relax

  _____

  7. take life easy

  _____

  8. sit in the yard

  _____

  9. drive to the country

  _____

  10. seem happy

  _____

Part 2: *Wintertime*

Example: wear a heavy coat
   In the wintertime, everyone wears a heavy coat.

1. need boots and gloves
   _____

2. have trouble driving
   _____

3. stay inside a lot
   _____

4. go skiing
   _____

5. get sick
   _____

6. have accidents
   _____

7. play in the snow
   _____

8. stay at home and sleep a lot
   _____

9. throw snowballs
   _____

10. have fun in the snow
   _____

Please *rewrite* each of the following sentences two times. *Use* **becomes** and **gets** in place of **is.** At the end of each sentence, *use* **"in the (season)".** (*Fill in* the word that is best for your climate.) Every sentence says something about the *weather.*

Example: It is warm.
          It becomes warm in the spring.
          It gets warm in the spring.

1. It is cool and pleasant.

    _____

    _____

2. It is hot and humid.

    _____

    _____

3. It is cold and rainy.

    _____

    _____

4. It is sunny.

    _____

    _____

5. It is hot and dry.

    _____

    _____

6. It is dark and cloudy.

    _____

    _____

7. It is cool and foggy.

    _____

    _____

Please *choose* **verbs** from the following list to complete the sentences below. *Use* each verb only one time. The grammar and the **meaning** will help you decide. Every sentence says something about the **weather** and the **seasons** of the year.

snows	turns	rains
gets	are	fall
drops	comes	shines
bloom		

1. In the springtime, the grass _____ green.

2. Flowers _____ in the spring.

3. The sun _____ almost every day.

4. In the fall, leaves _____ from the trees.

5. In the spring, everything _____ alive.

6. In the winter, the temperature _____ to zero.

7. It sometimes _____ and we need to carry umbrellas.

8. It _____ very, very cold in the winter.

9. It _____ a lot in the winter and the children like to throw snowballs.

10. There _____ four seasons: spring, summer, fall, and winter.

Please *rewrite* the following sentences. *Change* the **word order**. *Put* the last part of each sentence first. Don't forget to *use* a comma after each part that you put first.

Example: There are four seasons in this part of the United States.
                In this part of the United States, there are four seasons.

1. Everything comes alive in the springtime.

   _____

2. The sun shines almost every day in the summertime.

   _____

3. The leaves turn orange and red in the fall.

   _____

4. It gets hot and humid in the summer.

   _____

5. The air is cool and pleasant after the rain is over.

   _____

6. It snows a lot in the wintertime.

   _____

7. It gets very, very cold in the winter.

   _____

8. People need to wear heavy coats when they go outside.

   _____

9. There are different activities for each season.

   _____

10. There are four seasons in Detroit.

   _____

Notes and questions on the *organization* of Reading 8.

Part A: *Paragraphs*

In Reading 8, the writer explains the weather in a certain region. In Detroit, where the writer lives, there are four seasons. Therefore, you might expect six paragraphs: an introduction, one paragraph for each season, and a conclusion. However, there are only five paragraphs. The following questions will help you see the *system of paragraphs* in Reading 8:

1. Where does the writer introduce the topic? How does the writer introduce the topic?

2. Where does the writer explain each season? Does the writer combine any seasons in order to explain? If so, how?

3. Where does the writer end the explanation of the seasons? Is this the end of the body, then? What follows?

4. How does the writer conclude the composition? What signals the conclusion?

You can see that there are three basic parts in Reading 8: an *introduction* (the first paragraph), a *body* (the three following paragraphs), and a *conclusion* (the last paragraph). This is the usual *system of paragraphs* in composition writing. The paragraphs form the three basic parts. *Be sure* that you understand the system. *Be sure* that you understand how the paragraphs can form these parts and work together in a system.

Part B: *Order*

The following questions will help you understand the *order of information* in Reading 8:

1. Does the writer explain the organization of the topic *weather*? How? Where?

2. How many sub-topics, or classes, does the writer give you?

3. Does the writer give equal space to each sub-topic?

4. Which seasons are explained first? Which ones follow? Is another order possible? If the writer talks first about spring and fall, why is summer next?

In Unit 3, you learned about *classification*. It is a division into sub-topics, or classes. *Weather* is a good topic to classify. Can you think of others? Now, *go on* to Model 8.

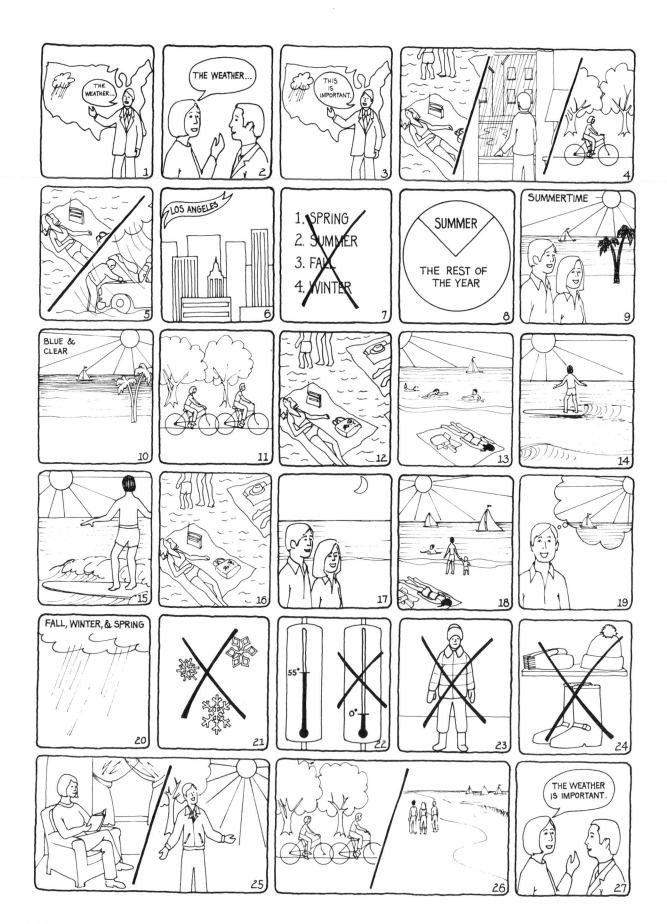

The Weather in Los Angeles

The weather! The weather! The weather! Don't people talk about anything else? It is true that the weather is important to us. Our activities change with the weather. Our lives may become easy or difficult. I live in Los Angeles and Los Angeles is not like many parts of the United States. Here, we don't really have four seasons. We have summer and we have the rest of the year.

Summertime is fun time. The sun shines almost every day and the sky is blue and clear. People come alive and spend a lot of time outside. It gets hot during the day and everyone goes to the beach. There, they swim or lie in the sun. Many young people go surfing. They try to stand up on their big surfboards and ride over the waves. The beaches are very crowded during the weekend. In the evening, the temperature drops and it is cool and pleasant. In the summertime, people take life easy. I love summer!

Fall, winter, and spring are really one big season. It rains a little, but it doesn't snow. The temperature is cool, but it rarely gets cold. A person doesn't need a heavy coat. Boots, hats, and gloves are never necessary. People spend more time inside, but it is still pleasant outside. I and my friends go for bicycle rides or long walks on the beach.

In conclusion, the weather is very important to us. Our lives change with the weather. In Los Angeles, we only have one big change and that is summer. I like the different activities of summertime. Why can't we have summer all year?

Instructions for student's composition:

1. Write a composition about the weather in your home country or home state. Classify the weather into seasons. Describe the seasons. Write your composition on 8½ x 11 loose-leaf notebook paper.

2. Write four, five, or six paragraphs. The number of paragraphs depends on the number of seasons. You can combine seasons that are similar. Don't forget to indent for each paragraph and leave margins. Put the following information in your paragraphs:

> First paragraph — Introduce the topic. Is the weather important? Which part of the world are you writing about? How many seasons are there?
>
> Paragraphs 2, 3 (4, 5) — Describe each season.
>
> Last paragraph — Conclude with general statements. What are your feelings?

3. Take what you need from Model 8. Let it help you with grammar, vocabulary, ideas, and organization.

4. Your composition should look like this:

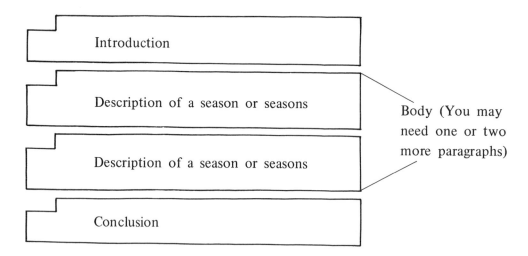

Unit 9

Grammatical Focus: Two-word verbs
Modals: *will, can, might, should, must*

Composition Focus: Description

Organizational Focus: Classification (human characteristics: physical traits and personality traits)
Balance of contrasts

John and I

My brother, John, and I are very different. We look different and we act different. Most people cannot believe that we are brothers. They think that we might be cousins or friends.

I look like our mother. John looks like our father. Therefore, he has black hair and I have blond hair. He is tall and I am short. I cannot play basketball with him. He always wins! John is thin. I will not say that I am fat, but I am a little heavy. John's eyes are good, but I cannot see a thing without my glasses. John is handsome. We should never go to a dance together because all the girls want to dance with him.

Our personalities are very different also. I am a very careful person. John can be very careless. For example, I look over my homework before class; John never does. I write down everything that the teacher says. Then, John will ask to copy my notes! I hand in my homework on time; John is usually late. When I fill out a form, I give all the necessary information. John, on the other hand, leaves out important information. Around the house, I am very neat and tidy. John is very messy. I always put away my things. John might pick up his clothes once in a while! I throw away things that I don't need. John throws everything in his closet. What a messy closet! You should never try to open his closet door. John and I can never agree on anything. If I turn on the T.V., he says that I should turn it off. If I turn up the radio, he says that I should turn it down.

How can we be brothers? I don't understand it. We are very different and we must live with our differences. We might argue and disagree, but we love each other. We are proud to be brothers.

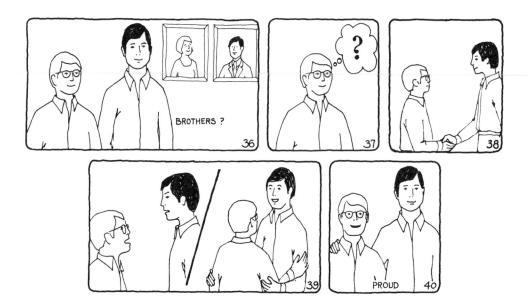

Please *rewrite* the following sentences. *Use* the **modal auxiliary** in parentheses. *Put* it into your sentence. *Make* any necessary changes.

Example: Most people don't believe that we are brothers. (cannot)
              Most people cannot believe that we are brothers.

 1. They think that we are cousins. (might)

     _____

 2. I do not say that I am fat. (will not)

     _____

 3. I don't see a thing without my glasses. (can't)

     _____

 4. We never go to a dance together. (should)

     _____

 5. John is very careless. (can)

     _____

 6. John picks up his clothes once in a while. (might)

     _____

 7. John asks to copy my notes. (will)

     _____

 8. You never open his closet door. (should)

     _____

 9. John and I never agree. (can)

     _____

10. We live with our differences. (must)

     _____

Please *translate* the **meaning** of the italicized part of each sentence. The meaning centers on the **modal auxiliary**. *Choose* the correct translation below each sentence. If you have trouble, *find* the sentence in Reading 9. *Reread* it and *think* about the **context**.

1. Most people *cannot* believe that we are brothers.
    a.   do not
    b.   find it impossible to
    c.   don't want to
    d.   will not

2. They think that *we might be* cousins or friends.
    a.   it is probable that we are
    b.   we are
    c.   we think that we are
    d.   it is possible that we are

3. I *cannot* see a thing without my glasses.
    a.   am unable to
    b.   don't want to
    c.   find it difficult to
    d.   don't like to

4. *We should never* go to a dance together because all the girls want to dance with him.
    a.   it is not possible for us to
    b.   we don't have to
    c.   it is a bad idea for us to
    d.   we are unable to

5. Then, *John will ask* to copy my notes.
    a.   John is able
    b.   John finds it possible
    c.   it is a good idea for John to ask
    d.   it always follows that John asks

6. *You should never* open his closet door.
   a. it is impossible for you to
   b. it is not a good idea for you to
   c. you do not have permission to
   d. you are not able to

7. We *must* live with our differences.
   a. find it necessary to
   b. are going to
   c. have permission to
   d. are able to

Please *rewrite* each sentence or request below. *Change* the **noun object** to a **pronoun object**. *Separate* the **two parts of the verb** and *put* the pronoun object between.

Example: Please turn down the radio.
             Please turn it down.

1. Would you please hand in your homework?

   _____

2. You should put away your notes before the examination.

   _____

3. Will you please turn up the T.V.?

   _____

4. Could you please fill out his form?

   _____

5. Throw away those old newspapers, please.

   _____

6. You must write down this telephone number.

   _____

7. Please pick up those pieces of paper.

   _____

8. You should look over these apples before you buy them.

   _____

9. You should turn on the news now if you want to watch it.

   _____

10. Please turn off that light when you finish studying.

   _____

Please *rewrite* the sentences below. Rewrite only the sentences that need **two-word verbs.** *Take out* the italicized part and *put in* a two-word verb. The italicized part gives the **meaning.** *Choose* from the list of two-word verbs below. *Use* each verb only one time.

pick up	put away	turn off
fill out	hand in	turn up
write down	throw away	turn down
look over	turn on	

Example: I need to *lower the volume on* the radio. The baby can't sleep.
            I need to turn down the radio.

1. I should *give* my homework *to the teacher.* She expects to have it before we leave class.

    _____

2. You must *note* all the important information. You will need to have it in your notebook in order to study for the examination.

    _____

3. You may *dispose of* these old shoes. I don't need them any more. They are no good.

    _____

4. You should *raise the volume on* the radio. I can't hear it.

    _____

5. Will you please *complete* this application? We need your name, address, and social security number.

    _____

6. You should *examine* your answers. Look for careless mistakes.

    _____

7. Would you please *start* the T.V. It's time for the news.

    _____

8. Please *remove* these pencils *from the floor.* Someone might fall.

    _____

9. Please *stop* the radio. I can't sleep.

    _____

10. Children should learn to *place* their toys *in the proper spot* after they finish play-
    ing.

    _____

Notes and questions on the *organization* of Reading 9.

Part A: *Paragraphs*

Reading 9 describes two people. There are four paragraphs. *Look back* at those paragraphs to *identify* the three basic parts: *introduction, body,* and *conclusion.* The following questions will help you be sure:

1. Where does the writer introduce the topic? What is the topic?
2. Where does the main part begin? Where does it end? How long is it? How is it divided?
3. Where does the conclusion begin? How does the writer conclude the composition? What does the writer do with the topic in the conclusion?

Part B: *Order*

Look back at the introduction to the composition. Do you know what kind of order to expect in the body of the composition? Does the writer tell you? The following questions will help you be sure about the *order of information* in Reading 9:

1. The specific topic is *John and I.* What kind of topic is that? How can that kind of topic be organized? (Do you remember Unit 3?) Into how many sub-topics does the writer divide the topic? What are the sub-topics?
2. Which sub-topic comes first in the body of the composition? Which comes second? Does it matter? It doesn't really, does it?

Do you remember that this kind of organization is called *classification*? In Reading 9, there is something else happening within each class, or sub-topic. *Look* closely. Do you see *black–blond, tall–short, thin–heavy,* etc.? *Notice* that each characteristic is followed by the opposite characteristic. There is a balance. Let's call it a *balance of contrasts.* Sometimes the contrasts are indirect as, for example, in the last sentence of the second paragraph. The contrast is between *handsome–not so handsome. Pick out* contrasts in the third paragraph. Then, *go on* to Model 9 to see the same techniques in operation.

Kim and I

My sister, Kim, and I are opposites in every way. We look different and we act different. It is hard to believe that we are sisters. Some people think that we are cousins. Others think that we might be roommates.

I look like my grandmother. Kim doesn't look like anyone in the family. Perhaps our mother brought the wrong baby home from the hospital! That could explain the differences! Kim is short, while I am tall. She has a very slight build and I have a medium build. We can never wear each other's clothes. My hair is red; hers is brown. I have green eyes; hers are blue. She must wear glasses, but I can see well without them. People say that we are both pretty, but we are pretty in different ways.

Our personalities are different, too. Kim likes music and can play the piano well. She can pick up a piece of music, look it over, and play it immediately. The family thinks that she should take up music full-time. However, she wants to become an engineer. As for me, I can't play anything. I have no musical ability. I am, however, a wonderful medical secretary. I can fill out insurance forms neatly and accurately. I can look over the doctor's instructions and understand them easily. I can write down important information quickly. The doctor gives me important responsibility. She says that I run the office, not her. Kim could never do my job and I could never be a musician or an engineer.

Our differences sometimes cause us problems. Kim and I often argue and disagree. However, we love each other and we must learn to accept our differences. In short, we will be sisters for a long, long time!

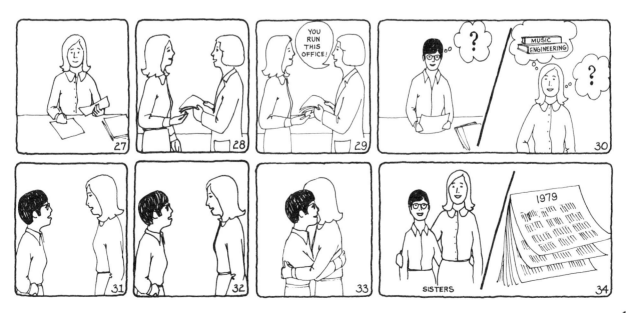

131

Instructions for student's composition:

1. Write a composition about yourself and someone you know. Choose someone who is very different from you. Write about the differences. Always give your composition a title. Write your composition on 8½ x 11 loose-leaf notebook paper.

2. Write four paragraphs. Remember to indent and leave margins. Put the following information in your paragraphs:

    Paragraph 1 — What are you writing about? Who are you writing about? Say that you are dividing the topic into *looks* and *actions*. What do people think?

    Paragraph 2 — Describe the differences in physical appearance.

    Paragraph 3 — Describe the differences in personality.

    Paragraph 4 — Conclude with general statements. Do the differences cause problems? How do you feel about the differences?

3. Take what you need from Model 9. Let it help you with organization, grammar, ideas, and vocabulary.

4. Your composition should look like this:

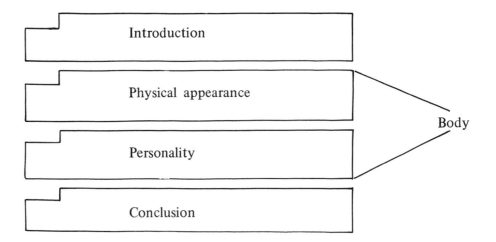

Unit 10

Grammatical Focus: Subject + Verb (present perfect tense)
Expressions of comparison

Composition Focus: Narration

Organizational Focus: Classification (time: activities/sights and knowledge)

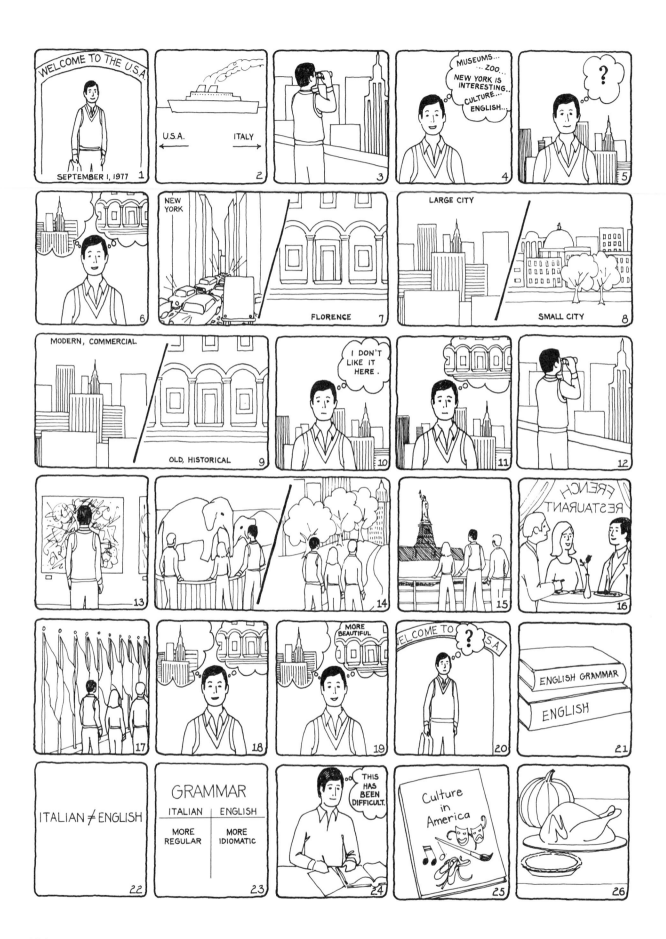

My Stay in the United States

I arrived in the United States on September 1, 1977. I came here from Italy by boat. Since my arrival, I have seen many new and interesting sights. I have also learned a lot.

New York was very strange to me at the beginning. It was very different from Florence, my hometown. New York seemed dirtier and noisier than Florence. It certainly looked larger. New York seemed much more modern and commercial than old, historical Florence. Since then, I have become acquainted with New York and I like it better. I have visited the Museum of Modern Art and the Metropolitan Museum of Art. My friends and I have enjoyed many afternoons at the Bronx Zoo and in Central Park. We have ridden the Staten Island Ferry. We have eaten in different restaurants. We have toured the United Nations Building. Now, I think that New York is as interesting as Florence. It will never be as beautiful, but no city will ever equal Florence!

When I arrived, there was a lot that I didn't understand. Since then, I have learned a lot of English. It has been difficult because Italian is very different from English. Italian grammar seems more regular and less idiomatic. Nevertheless, I have improved my English. I have also learned a lot about American culture. I had Thanksgiving dinner with an American family last November. Recently, I have gone to several jazz concerts. I still have a lot to learn, but I am beginning to feel more comfortable in this country.

I plan to stay in New York for several more years. I hope to travel more before I return to my country. I will be happy to return home, but I will not return home the same person. I will be older and wiser and I will be more fluent in English!

Pretend that you are the person who wrote Reading 10; in other words, you are "I". Please *answer* the following question by completing the sentences below. *Use* the **present perfect tense** with **I have** + Past Participle.

Question: What have you seen, done, and learned since you arrived in the United States?

Example: become acquainted with New York
           I have become acquainted with New York.

1. visit the Museum of Modern Art

   _____

2. go to the Metropolitan Museum of Art

   _____

3. enjoy many afternoons at the Bronx Zoo

   _____

4. spend many afternoons in Central Park

   _____

5. ride the Staten Island Ferry

   _____

6. eat in different restaurants

   _____

7. tour the United Nations Building

   _____

8. learn a lot of English

   _____

9. improve my English

   _____

10. learn a lot about American culture

_____

11. have Thanksgiving dinner with an American family

_____

12. go to several jazz concerts

_____

Compare New York City and Florence, Italy. *Use* the following information to make your statements of *comparison*. The information comes from Reading 10.

Example: New York — Florence (different)
              New York is different from Florence.

1. New York — Florence (dirtier)

   _____

2. New York — Florence (noisier)

   _____

3. New York — Florence (more modern)

   _____

4. New York — Florence (as interesting)

   _____

5. New York — Florence (more commercial)

   _____

6. New York — Florence (larger)

   _____

7. Florence — New York (older)

   _____

8. Florence — New York (more beautiful)

   _____

9. Florence — New York (more historical)

   _____

10. Florence — New York (more familiar to me)

    _____

The italicized part of each following sentence refers the reader to another part of the same sentence or to another sentence in Reading 10. What is the *reference*? Please *circle* the letter a, b, or c to show the correct reference. *Find* each sentence in Reading 10 in order to decide.

1. Since *my arrival*, I have seen many new and interesting sights.

   What does *my arrival* refer to?
      a.   going to see the sights of New York
      b.   becoming acquainted with New York
      c.   coming to the United States

2. *It* was very different from Florence, my hometown.

   What does *it* refer to?
      a.   New York
      b.   Italy
      c.   the United States

3. It certainly looked *larger*.

   What does *larger* refer to? *Larger* than what?
      a.   New York
      b.   Florence
      c.   the United States

4. *It* will never be as beautiful, but no city will ever equal Florence!

   What does *it* refer to?
      a.   Central Park
      b.   the United Nations Building
      c.   New York

5. *It* has been difficult because Italian is very different from English.

   What does *it* refer to?
      a.   arriving here
      b.   not understanding
      c.   learning English

6. I still have a lot to *learn,* but I am beginning to feel more comfortable in this country.

   What does *learn* refer to? *Learn* about what?

        a.   American culture

        b.   Thanksgiving

        c.   jazz

Please *complete* the following sentences. *Take* the expression that you need from below each sentence or group of sentences. The expressions **connect** the ideas in each sentence or in each group of sentences. The **meaning** and the **grammar** will help you.

1. I came here in September, 1977. _____ my arrival, I have seen and done a lot.

    a. during
    b. since
    c. after
    d. before

2. _____ , I didn't like New York. I felt homesick for Florence. Now, I like New York much better.

    a. as a result
    b. however
    c. afterwards
    d. at first

3. New York will never be as beautiful as Florence, _____ no city will ever equal Florence.

    a. but
    b. so
    c. and
    d. when

4. Studying English has been difficult because Italian is very different from English. _____ , I have improved.

    a. therefore
    b. then
    c. nevertheless
    d. furthermore

5. _____ I arrived, there was a lot that I didn't understand.

    a. when
    b. if
    c. but
    d. so

6. I hope to travel more _____ I return to my country.

    a.   however

    b.   before

    c.   because

    d.   and

Notes and questions on the *organization* of Reading 10.

Part A: *Paragraphs*

Reading 10 tells a story of someone's stay in the United States. There are four paragraphs. *Look back* at those paragraphs. *Identify* the three basic parts within the **system of paragraphs:** *introduction, body,* and **conclusion.** *Tell why* you think so.

Part B: *Order*

The title of Reading 10 suggests a period of time. There is an important date in the introduction. You might, therefore, expect the **order of information** to be chronological. However, it is not. The following questions will help you decide what it is:

1. What does the writer say about the time since his arrival? How is it divided in the introduction? What are the sub-topics?
2. Which sub-topic does the writer discuss first? How does the writer get into that sub-topic?
3. Which sub-topic is next? How many examples does the writer give within that sub-topic?
4. How does the writer conclude the discussion of the sub-topics? Does the writer add new information?

Reading 10 uses **classification** as a tool to organize the information. The writer organizes the contents of time. **Contrasts** help to show change and progression within the period of time.

Take a moment to *review* all the different ways to order information. Then, *go on* to Model 10.

My Stay in the United States

July 15, 1978 was an important day! On that day, I arrived in the United States. I came here from Mexico by plane. Since my arrival, I have seen and done a lot. I have also learned many new things.

At first, I didn't like Ann Arbor. It was very different from Mexico City, my hometown. It seemed quieter and less interesting. It certainly looked neater and cleaner, but it also seemed less sophisticated. I felt homesick for the excitement of Mexico City. Since then, I have become more acquainted with Ann Arbor and I like it better. I have visited all parts of the University of Michigan campus. A friend and I have taken bicycle rides in the country. We have visited some of the farms and small towns in the area. We have driven over to Lake Michigan. Now, I think that this area is almost as interesting as Mexico City.

When I arrived, there was a lot that I still had to learn. Since then, I have improved my English. It hasn't been easy because English is a difficult language. It seems less regular and more idiomatic than Spanish. Nevertheless, I have done well. Now, I can understand a lot. I understand American culture much better now, too. Since my arrival, I have gone to some parties here on campus. I have also learned to dance. I have seen a lot of American movies. Last Christmas, I spent several days with an American family. I still have a lot to learn, but I am beginning to feel more at home here.

I plan to stay in Ann Arbor for two more years. I hope to visit Los Angeles and San Francisco sometime next summer. I hope to see most of the United States before I return home. I will be happy to return home, but everything will be different for me. I will certainly be different! I will be more educated, older, and wiser than when I left.

Instructions for student's composition:

1. Write a composition about your stay in the United States or your life in the city where you live. Divide your composition into two parts: what you have seen/done and what you have learned. Give your composition a title. Write on 8½ x 11 paper.

2. Write four paragraphs. Remember to indent and leave margins. Put the following information in your paragraphs:

   Paragraph 1 – When did you arrive? How did you come and where did you come from? Show that you are dividing the topic into two parts: *seen/done* and *learned.*

   Paragraph 2 – Describe the beginning. What was different between the old place and the new place? What have you seen/done in the new place?

   Paragraph 3 – What have you learned in the new place?

   Paragraph 4 – Conclude with your future plans. Tell about your possible return home.

3. Use Model 10. Let it help you with grammar, ideas, vocabulary, and organization.

4. Your composition should look like this:

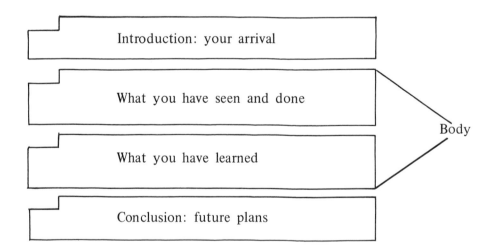

146

STUDENT'S NOTES

STUDENT'S NOTES

STUDENT'S NOTES